Visual Introduction to Bucks Point Lace

Geraldine Stott

B.T. Batsford Ltd, London

By the same author (together with Bridget M. Cook)
and published by Batsford:

The Book of Bobbin Lace Stitches (1980)
100 Traditional Bobbin Lace Patterns (1982)
Introduction to Bobbin Lace Stitches (1983)

My grateful thanks to all my students and friends for their help, support and
advice, especially Mrs L. Meteyard, for introducing me to lace, Mrs D. Fudge and
Mrs D. Carr. Special thanks to my 'Friday' class who have solemnly plodded their
way right through the book as intended – cover to cover. Congratulations to Mrs
Anne Varley for making the Baby Bonnet Back sample. I also wish to express my
gratitude to Miss Elsie Turnham's nieces for allowing me to use her Threepenny
Spot pattern.

First published 1985

Reprinted 1990, 1992

This paperback edition first published 1995

ISBN 0 7134 4372 3

Typeset by Servis Filmsetting Ltd, Manchester
and printed in Hong Kong.

for the publisher
B.T. Batsford
4 Fitzhardinge Street
London W1H 0AH

Patricia Elberum

CONTENTS

Contents

INTRODUCTION

The patterns have been selected to introduce at least one new technique for each design. They have also been put in order of difficulty: I suggest you start with the Little Fan and progress and learn as shown. I also strongly recommend you work the *large scale prickings first*. It may not look good lace, but you will be able to see what is happening, which is almost impossible with the large number of pins at the correct pricking size; it also gets you used to the thin thread and pins.

Thread

I have used throughout Mr Piper's polycotton no. 2/80, unless otherwise stated. Unity 150 and Brok 100/2 or 100/3 can also be used. For the gimp I used D.M.C. Coton à Broder 18. Most patterns in this book have five holes per centimetre (12 and a half holes per inch) measuring along the footside. It is fun when you are more experienced to make even finer Bucks Point lace using a reducing photocopier. I use Brok no. 120/2 or 140/2 for 6½ per centimetre or 16 holes per inch and Coton a Bròder nos. 20 or 25 for gimps.

Conservation of thread

It makes me weep to see the yards of curly thread that has to be thrown away because of misjudgement of lengths; we all fear running out before the end, so wind on too much. A handy rule of thumb: four times the length of your work is usually sufficient. I recommend, if you intend doing many little practice pieces, that you wind a lot of thread on to one bobbin, then only wind enough for the sample from this bobbin on to its pair bobbin. This is the method I have used for all my book samples.

Prickings

From experience I find there are many lacemakers who have neither pens, skills nor time to prick and draw out complicated Bucks Point patterns. The following is the method I use constantly: photocopy your pattern (acceptable only for your own personal use); cut out pricking; cut out card slightly larger; cover pricking and card with sticky-backed, transparent, *coloured plastic film*; rub with wire wool to remove the shine.

If you have trouble seeing through coloured plastic film, the following is the way to make a correct pricking: firmly stick your copy right down one side only with tape (creating a flap); prick through the outline of the motif inside the gimp; carefully lift up your copy flap and draw in gimp line with a fine pen; smooth copy back, then prick in fillings, then grounds; when all has been transferred to the card remove tape and copy.

I strongly recommend temporary sticking, rather than pinning – pinholes are inclined to enlarge and therefore distort the final copy.

Pins

Traditional, long, fine brass pins 55 mm × 30.

Hanging on in order

Always hang on in order unless otherwise stated.

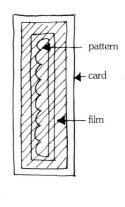

- pattern
- card
- film

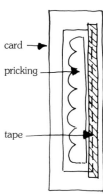

- card
- pricking
- tape

hanging on in order

hanging on in pairs

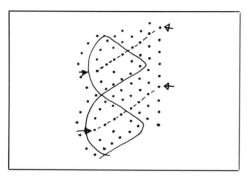

Hanging on in pairs

Observe your pattern. Find the longest complete row and count number of pinholes, discounting headside and footside pins. In this instance there are 7. Add 4 for footside; add 2 for headside. Therefore 13 pairs are needed.

Always *twist twice round a pin* unless otherwise stated.

Knots

Knots are taboo in Bucks Point lace. Manoeuvre the thread that is running out to some whole-stitch feature if possible, then work side by side with a new pair for a short while, before throwing out the old pair and continuing with the new pair.

Tension/bobbin moving

Moving your bobbins from side to side helps settle the threads down and therefore helps tension. If you use the flat of your hand to sweep the bobbins gently to and fro there is less likelihood of bobbins getting misplaced.

Cover cloths

These are absolutely essential to cover your work every moment you are not working. Put the cover cloth on your knee while working, then it is impossible to forget to cover the work as you leave the pillow.

Throughout, I have drawn the diagrams to show the way I work the lace. This does not mean it's the only way; they are there for your guidance and when you have mastered this method you can experiment with others. **There are no right and wrong ways, just the way that suits you best.**

COLOUR-CODING KEY

—— Red lines indicate stitches to be worked in whole stitch

—— Blue lines indicate stitches to be worked in half stitch

—— Thin black lines indicate weaving

▬▬ Thick black lines indicate gimp threads

 Little dashes on diagrams show number of twists

▼ Start of a new gimp or gimp pair

 Finish of a gimp pair

+ Start of a new pair

 Taking out of a pair

ABBREVIATIONS

w.s.	whole stitch
h.s.	half stitch
h.c.s.	honeycomb stitch
p.g.s.	point ground stitch
tw.1	twist once
tw.2	twist twice
tw.3	twist three times
L.H.	left hand
R.H.	right hand
B.P.L.	Buckingham Point lace
⊙	temporary pin

1 LITTLE FAN

Bobbins 11 pairs – **Gimps** 1 single

Introducing – temporary pins; catchpin stitch; point ground stitch and single gimp

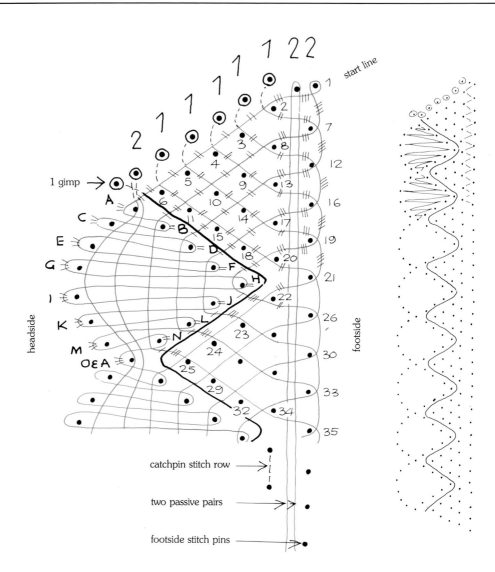

1 gimp →

start line

catchpin stitch row ⟶

two passive pairs ⟶

footside stitch pins ⟶

headside

footside

This is an old, very traditional first Buckingham Point Lace pattern.
Aim for gentle curving lines of fan passives. Large loops and straight lines
are not desirable.
See page 10 for an ingenious use for this pattern.

Temporary pins ⊙

Help give a neat start to your work. Hang appropriate pairs on pins above start line; when using an existing pricking, find convenient holes above your chosen start line.

> **Point ground stitch** – (**p.g.s.**) h.s., tw.2 and pin between pairs. *Do not cover.* The most important stitch in Bucks Point lace.

> **Footside stitch** – w.s., tw.3 and tw.4* two outside pairs, pin under both, w.s. L.H. pair back through passive pairs.

* I always like to give the outside pair an extra twist – this counteracts the natural curving tendency of the lace.

> **Catchpin stitch** – tw.3, pin under, h.s., tw.2 (point ground stitch) with pair from above. *Do not pin.*

Gimps

Thick outlining thread – a very distinctive feature of Bucks Point Lace. Whichever direction the gimps travel, I find this is the best method: pick up L.H. bobbin with left hand, and pop gimp through the gap.

Pairs must always be twisted before and after gimps. Traditionally it was tw.2 before and after, but I prefer:

> tw.1 before w.s.   tw.2 before h.c.s.   tw.3 before p.g.s.

START HERE

Tw.1 then w.s. 2 pairs together at **1**, tw.3 and tw.4 as * above; w.s. L.H. pair through 2 passive pairs, work catchpin stitch at **2** and p.g.s. at **3**, **4**, **5** and **6**. Carefully remove temporary pins and let threads down to start line. W.s. pair left at **2** through passive pairs, tw.3, work footside at **7**.

Standard working

Work catchpin stitch at **8** and p.g.s. at **9**, **10** and **11**. Work pair left at 8 through passive pairs, tw.3, work footside at 12. Work catchpin stitch at **13** and p.g.s. at **14** and **15**. Work pair left at 13 through passive pairs, tw.3, work footside at **16**. Work catchpin stitch at **17** and p.g.s. at **18**. Work pair left at 17 through passive pairs, tw.3, work footside at **19**. Work catchpin stitch at **20**. Work pair left at 20 through passive pairs, work footside at **21**. *Stop!* Take gimp through pairs from 6, 11, 15, 18 and 20. T.w.1 all 5 pairs.

Whole-stitch fan

With L.H. pair from 6, w.s. through 2 new pairs, tw.3, pin at **A**. (Carefully let pairs from temporary pin down.) W.s. back and forth, tw.3 outside edge and tw.2 elsewhere, picking up a new pair until widest point of fan **H** then leaving out one pair each row until pin **O** is reached, tw.1 pairs from H, J, L and N, take gimp through them, tw.3 these pairs.

Now you are ready to start your new p.g.s. triangle: w.s. pair from 21 through passives tw.3, now work **22** as 8, **23** as 9, etc.

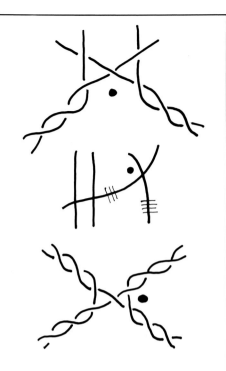

2 HONEYCOMB GROUND

Bobbins 13 pairs   **Introducing** – honeycomb stitch; picots

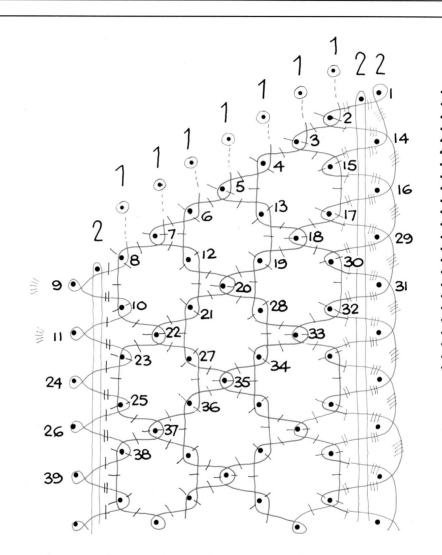

Sometimes there is confusion at the straight edges (inside passives) of this ground; try to visualise h.c. ground as a series of hexagons.

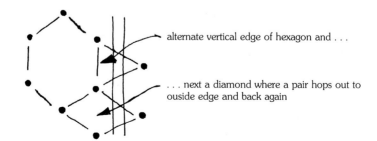

alternate vertical edge of hexagon and . . .

. . . next a diamond where a pair hops out to ouside edge and back again

> **Honeycomb stitch** – (h.c.s.) – h.s., tw.1, pin, h.s., tw.1

As honeycomb stitch and point ground stitch are made out of half stitch, they are very unstable and cannot be pulled tight as all whole-stitch based stitches. I recommend you get into the habit of stroking your bobbins downwards gently as often as possible. This helps keep a good tension.

Footside stitch (for honeycomb only)

W.s. tw.3 and tw.4 outside pairs, pin under both, w.s. L.H. pair through passives, tw.*2* (honeycomb is basically tw.2 throughout).

> **Picots** – tw.5, with pin in right hand, put pin on top of left-hand thread and wind thread round in clockwise motion, put in pin, (hold threads up without tension). Take other thread in clockwise motion round same pin, tw.2, wriggle the threads to make the twists appear round the pin.

After picot has been made, push pin down more than usual – this leaves the next picot pin to be worked proud and it is therefore easier to wind the second thread round it. If you experiment with thick thread or string, you will note this method traps one set of threads within the other and it is therefore impossible for it to come untwisted.

START HERE

Hang pairs on temporary pins, passive pin and footside pin. W.s. 2 pairs together at **1** tw.3 and tw.4, w.s. L.H. pair through 2 passive pairs, tw.2. Honeycomb stitch at **2**, **3**, **4**, **5**, **6**, **7** and **8** with L.H. pair from last stitch and appropriate pair from above (sometimes called 'long row'). W.s. L.H. pair from 8 through passive pairs, picot at **9** w.s. back through passive pairs, tw.2. H.c.s. at **10** w.s. L.H. pair through passive pairs, picot **11** w.s. back through passive pairs, tw.2. H.c.s. at **12** and **13** with alternate pairs from last row (sometimes called 'short row'). W.s. pair left at 2 through passive pairs, work footside stitch at **14** h.c.s. at **15**. W.s. R.H. pair from 15 through passive pairs, work footside stitch at **16**.

Now you are ready to repeat the process, with a 'long row' starting at **17**.

Remember

Point ground stitch – h.s., tw.2.
Honeycomb stitch – h.s., tw.1, pin, h.s., tw.1.

3 SHEEP'S HEAD

Bobbins 13 pairs – **Gimps** 1 pair

Introducing – picots on curved headside

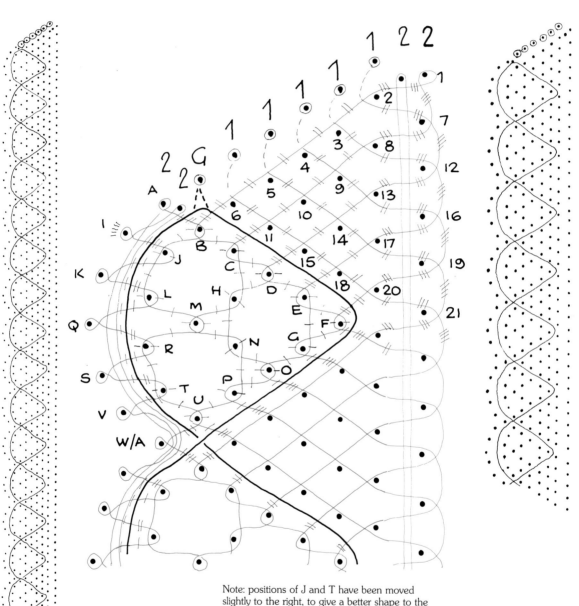

Note: positions of J and T have been moved slightly to the right, to give a better shape to the curve – a very common practice.

Double gimp – gimp pairs

Hang gimp on temporary pin above start line. Remove temporary pin after first honeycomb stitch (B) has been made. Always, when two gimps cross, *cross right over left.*

Picots

(i) W.s. 2 outside pairs through each other, work picot with L.H. pair, take this pair back through all heading pairs, tw.1, take through gimp.

(ii) Take pair from main pattern through gimp, tw.1, w.s. through heading pairs, picot, w.s. back through passives, tw.1, take through gimp.

(iii) Take pair from main pattern through gimp, tw.1, w.s. through heading pairs, picot, w.s. two outside pairs together, leave.

(iv) (Good place to start usually.) Hang 2 pairs on valley pin, tw.5 L.H. pair, w.s. through each other, take R.H. pair through rest of heading pairs, tw.1, take through gimp.

START HERE

Hang on pairs, as shown, on temporary pins, passive and footside pins.

P.g.s. triangle

Work **1** to **21** using techniques shown in Little Fan.

Honeycomb fan

Work pin **A** as (iv) above. Take R.H. gimp through pairs from 6, 11, 15, 18 and 20, tw.2 all 5 pairs. Tw.2 pairs from A, work h.c.s. at **B**, **C**, **D**, **E** and **F**. H.c.s. at **G** and **H** with alternate pairs from last row. Work picot (i) at **I**, tw.2, h.c.s. at **J**. Picot (ii) at **K**, tw.2. H.c.s. at **L**, **M**, **N** and **O**, then at **P**. Picot (ii) at **Q**, tw.2, h.c.s. at **R**, picot (ii) at **S**, tw.2. H.c.s. at **T** and **U**, picot (iii) at **V**. Picot ii at **W** (new A), tw.2. Tw. gimps over (right over left). Tw.3 pairs from F G O P U before starting again.

Remember

Point ground stitch – h.s., tw.2.
Honeycomb stitch – h.s., tw.1, pin h.s., tw.1.

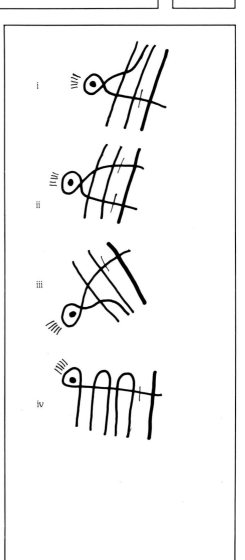

i

ii

iii

iv

4 HONEYCOMB RINGS

Bobbins 13 pairs – **Gimps** 1 pair   **Introducing** – honeycomb rings

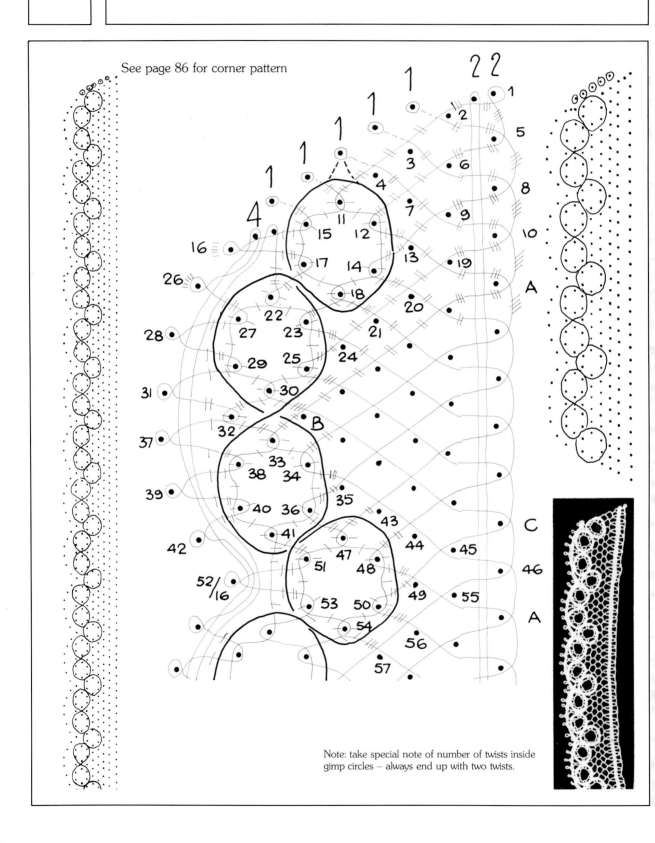

See page 86 for corner pattern

Note: take special note of number of twists inside gimp circles – always end up with two twists.

Honeycomb rings

These are very common in Bucks Point lace; basically, they are honeycomb hexagons surrounded by gimps. To achieve this it is necessary to work in the following sequence.

START HERE

Hang on pairs as shown, temporary pins, passive and footside pins.

.g.s. triangle

Work **1** to **10** using techniques shown in Little Fan.

First ring

Take gimp through 2 L.H. and R.H. pairs. T.w.2 all 4 pairs, h.c.s. **11** and **12**, take R.H. pair through gimp, tw.3, p.g.s. at **13**, take L.H. pair through gimp, tw.2, h.c.s. **14** and **15**. Take L.H. pair through gimp, tw.1, w.s. through 4 pairs, picot (ii) at **16**, w.s. back through 4 pairs, tw.1, through gimp, tw.2 h.c.s. **17** and **18**.

Overlapping gimps

Take gimps through pairs from 14 and 18, tw.3 both, and through pairs from 17 and 18. Cross gimps (right over left), take L.H. gimp through pairs from 18 and 17. (Please note *no twists* between overlapping gimps.) Then take through 1 pair from above, tw.2 all 3 pairs. Catchpin stitch and p.g.s. **19**, **20** and **21**.

Second ring

H.c.s. **22** and **23**, p.g.s. at **24** as 13 above, h.c.s. at **25**, picot (i) at **26** take through gimp, tw.2, h.c.s. at **27**, picot (ii) at **28**, take through gimp, tw.2, h.c.s. at **29** and **30**.

Crossed gimps

Take gimps through pairs from 25 and 30, and through pairs from 29 and 30. Cross gimps right over left. T.w.1 pair from 29, tw.2 L.H. pair from 30, w.3 pairs from 25 and 30, picot (ii) at **31**, but after returning through passives tw.2.

Outside h.c.s.

H.c.s. at **32** (quite a common feature in this form of lace).

P.g.s. triangle

Work triangle A – B – C as normal. Take gimp through 2 pairs to right and 1 pair to left, tw.2 all 3 pairs.

Third ring

33 to 41 as last ring (except picot [ii] at 37). After gimp, twist right over left, take R.H. gimp back through pairs from 41 and 36, tw.2, picot (iii) at 42, p.g.s., catchpin stitch and footside 43 to 46. Take R.H. gimp through 2 pairs to right, tw.2.

Now repeat from first ring again.

Remember

Point ground stitch – h.s., tw.2.
Honeycomb stitch – h.s., tw.1, pin, h.s., tw.1.

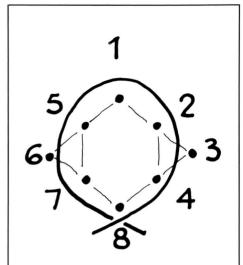

5 LITTLE FAN SACHET
Bobbins 11 pairs – **Gimps** 1 single   **Introducing** – finishing off

Best made on a round-domed pillow. Aim for a rounded *effect* at fan edge, *not* large loops. This is a *very* pretty adaptation of the traditional Little Fan pattern, that has many uses (see pages 2 and 3 for details).

Start line – hang pairs over gimp before starting. This is always the ideal spot to start.

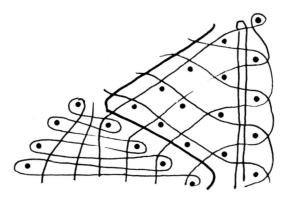

Finishing off

Clear the decks! Push down all pins near the join, both at beginning and end. I use a very clever invention that has an indentation one end to push down pins, and a two pronged fork the other to pull out the pins (see List of Suppliers). First and last fans and p.g.s. triangles *must* have pins all round. Lengthen all threads till at least 20 cm (8 in.) long.

START AT FOOTSIDE

Remove original first pin, insert a very fine crochet hook (0.60 mm) into this hole, pull through one thread of pair to be sewn, thread other thread (beads first is easiest) through loop created, pull tight, then tie in a reef knot, plus:

Reef knot and a half

(Again, beads first.) Right thread over and under left thread, then left thread over and under right thread. Repeat first move again. *Replace pin after every knotting* – very important for keeping good shape. Next, sew off at headside, then the internal pinholes. Some lacemakers recommend sewing back with needle after knotting, but this can look very unsightly, especially in the net.

The whole aim is a strong invisible join

After all the sewings and knottings, try the following method which works well for me:

a leave a pair at footside very long (use this to sew lace on to material);

b leave the weaver pair of fan long – sew this back along the gimp for strength;

c leave footside passives long – these can be woven back into beginning fairly invisibly;

d cut remaining threads and gimp threads 5 cm (2 in.) long for the time being;

e carefully remove all pins, except footside and headside pins; now you can cut close the short ends.

When sewing this lace on to your material you will find it much easier to work on an embroidery ring – circular sewings are notorious for bunching up in the middle.

Remember

Point ground stitch – h.s., tw.2.
Honeycomb stitch – h.s., tw.1, pin, h.s., tw.1.

6 NET AND TALLIES

Bobbins 18 pairs

Introducing – tallies in net; *point d'esprit* (little woven squares that decorate Bucks Point net; usually indicated on the prickings by no pinholes and/or large dots or squares).

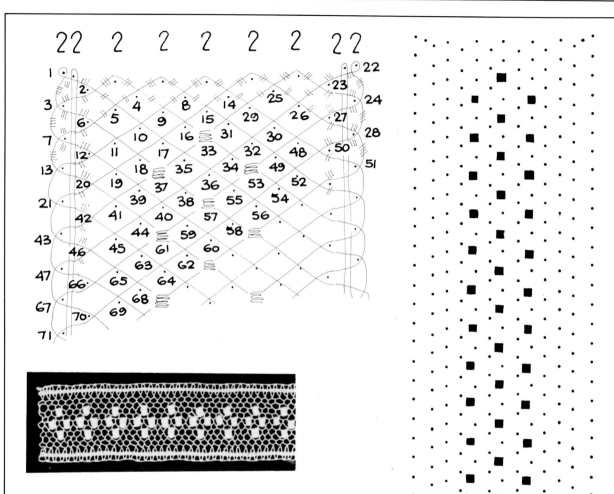

It is a good idea to use the very large-scale pricking and multiple colours in sewing cotton; this will help you to get to know where and how the threads travel which will be useful knowledge later – for instance, if you see a thread running out in your net, you will see that by 'cheating' (tw.3 instead of tw.2) the short thread can be made to travel away from the net into some feature where it is possible to bring in a new thread. *There must never be any knots in Bucks Point ground.*

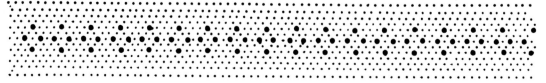

A prettier design

Straight starts

Have very few uses except they save time on practice pieces. Hang 2 pairs on each pin *in order*, tw.3 all except passive pairs.

START HERE

Work footside, catchpin stitch and point ground stitch as before, 1–32.

Tallies

There are many ways to make a tally. The following is the method I have found keeps its shape best for me.

Using 2 pairs from above, elongate the third thread from left and use it as a weaver (remember there must never be any tension on this thread throughout the weaving process).

Weave under thread to left and over next to left, return under, over, under. Pull weaver to right to create required size.

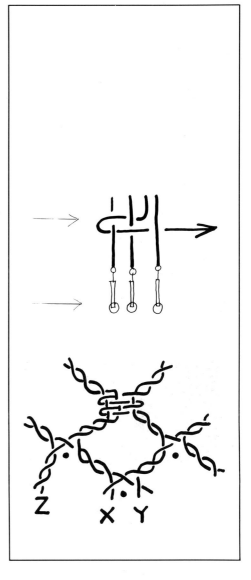

At the same time hold bobbins firmly with left hand while pulling.

Please *count* number of weaves back and forth so all tallies end up the same size. The ideal shape to end up with is exactly square.

When correct shape is achieved, fix it in position as follows. Still holding weaver in right hand, tw.3 2 left-hand threads, then the 2 right-hand threads, work a p.g.s. still holding the weaver, with pair to right; after pinning you can let go gently of the weaver thread, quickly work the p.g.s. to left of tally, then the stitch directly below the tally. Now your tally is fairly safe! If your tally falls crooked this can be corrected by gently pulling the threads X and/or Y.

Left-handed workers, should reverse the tally procedures – start and end on the left and leave the path clear on the left instead of the right.

For more detailed explanation of working theory and other methods, see page 13.

Remember

Point ground stitch – h.s., tw.2.
Honeycomb stitch – h.s., tw.1, pin, h.s., tw.1.

TALLIES, LEADWORKS, SPOTS, *POINT D'ESPRIT*, SQUARE PLAITS

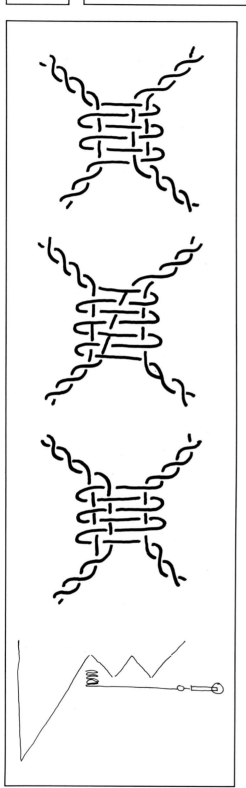

A survey of different methods; try them all and choose the method you like best.

Method 1 – begin and end on L.H. side

Method 2 – begin on L.H. side and end on R.H. side

Method 3 – begin and end on R.H. side (this is the method I find keeps its shape best)

I strongly advise you to try them *all* in the sampler.

Theory behind working sequence – always endeavour to keep your workspace clear; it is very difficult to work up a tight V section *and* keep a good shape. You will see by the numbering, I work as much as possible on the L.H. side but only just enough on the right, to keep the field clear for pulling weaver in a straight horizontal line without interference from pins.

There is a dear little baby bonnet in the Victoria & Albert Museum, London with 'Long Live The Babe' all worked in tallies!

Another traditional pattern

Prickings for glove handkerchief and full-size handkerchief.

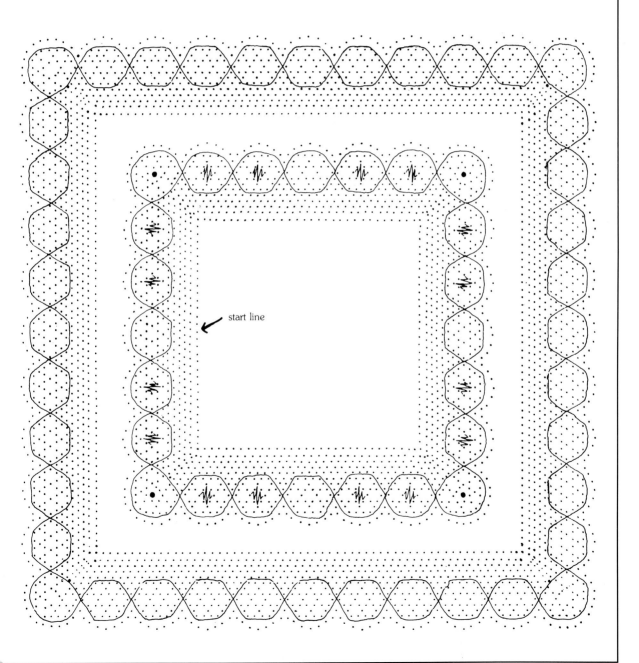

start line

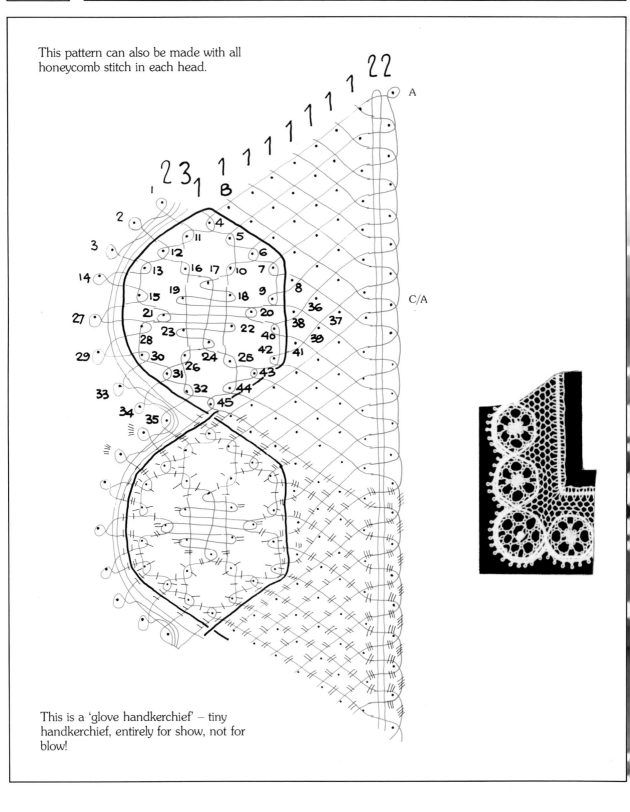

This pattern can also be made with all honeycomb stitch in each head.

This is a 'glove handkerchief' – tiny handkerchief, entirely for show, not for blow!

Mayflowers

These are a very common feature in honeycomb; they are whole-stitch diamonds in honeycomb. It does not matter which way the worker travels first, but it is essential always to keep working in the same direction throughout the piece of work.

Valley details

No picot and valley infill at this lowest point. With pair from honeycomb take through gimp, tw.1, w.s. through 4 pairs to outside edge, tw.5, pin, return through *3 pairs*.

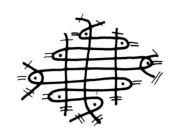

Infill

L.H. pair from bottom honeycomb take through gimp, tw.1, w.s. next 2 pairs to the left, tw.1 both these pairs. This method nicely fills up the gap at this point.

Catchpin stitch

At side of main feature. This helps the gimp shape, especially in floral work later.

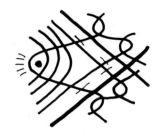

START HERE

Hang pairs on convenient pinholes above start line. * Work triangle A–B–C as usual. Picot (iv) at **1** (start only), picot (i) at **2** and **3**. Add 1 pair round gimp above 4 (start only). Take gimp through four R.H. and L.H. pairs, tw.2, h.c.s. **4**, **5**, **6** and **7**. Take R.H. pair from 7 through gimp, tw.3, catchpin stitch at **8**. Return through gimp, tw.2, h.c.s. **9**, **10**, **11**, **12** & **13**, picot (ii) at **14**, h.c.s. **15** and **16**.

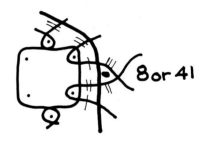

8 or 41

Mayflower

W.s., pin, w.s. at **17** w.s. back and forth twisting twice at each pinhole through **18**, **19**, **20** and **21** taking in a pair at each pin, then leaving out one pair from 20, 21, 22, 23 and 24 tw.2 all 6 pairs. H.c.s. **25** and **26**, picot (ii) **27**, h.c.s. **28**, picot (ii) **29**. H.c.s. **30**, **31** and **32**, picot (iii) **33** and **34**. Valley pin **35**, see above. P.g.s. **36** and **37**, catchpin stitch **38** and 8 above. P.g.s. **39**, h.c.s. **40**, catchpin stitch **41** as 8 above. H.c.s. **42**, **43**, **44** and **45** take gimp through 4 right-hand pairs. T.w.3 all 4 pairs, valley infill as above, twist gimps right over left. Repeat from * except A is a normal footside, of course!

Remember

Point ground stitch – h.s. tw.2.
Honeycomb stitch – tw.1, pin, h.s. tw.1.

7A PLUM PUDDING CORNER

Bobbins 17 pairs – **Gimps** 1 pair

Introducing – simple corners*

* Corners are comparatively modern – just straight lace gathered before

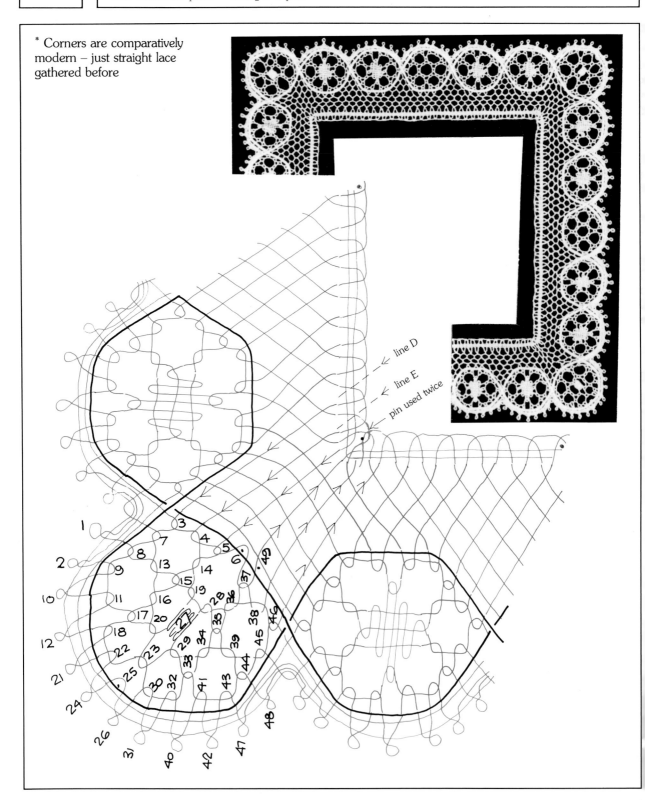

line D

line E

pin used twice

Plum Pudding corner

Work as normal until line E has been completed. Take pair from last catchpin through passives and work footside stitch, but *do not twist* outside pair. Take R.H. pair of passives through L.H. pair, tw.3, and p.g.s. with this pair up through 5 pairs, take gimp through 3 pairs from point ground, tw.2.

Picots and h.c.s. in order shown

Note: at **6** take the pair from 5 through gimp, tw.2, pin and return. W.s. pair from 24 through passives, tw.1, works through gimp, tw.2, pin and back out to next picot. At **27** work an extra large tally with L.H. pair from 19 and R.H. pair from 20, tw.2 after tally. Take 3 pairs from 37, 38 and 46 through gimp, tw.3, work catchpin stitch at **49**. Thereafter work p.g.s. down through next 4 pairs, w.s. through passive pair and leave in place. Take inner pair from corner pin through passives, tw.3, pin under and leave. Work p.g.s. down line (from 38) and work catchpin stitch with pair left on pin. Work through passives and round the pin again. To do this, make your stitch, carefully remove pin, and pin under both new pairs. Return L.H. pair through passives, tw.3, pin, work p.g.s. down last corner row (from 46) until this pin, work catchpin stitch.

Now you are ready to begin again as before

Handy hints

Keep the weaver of the tally long for the next few stitches to warn you still to be careful of this thread, so as to preserve the tally shape.

It will be noted when you have turned the corner you will have difficulty with the first few footside pins (the others are in the way, if you have correctly sloped all outside pins); therefore push first 2 cm ($\frac{3}{4}$ in.) of pins, except corner pin, right down.

8 THREEPENNY SPOT

Bobbins 18 pairs – **Gimps** 1 pair

Introducing – kat stitch – also called wire ground and French ground. A very pretty but little used stitch.

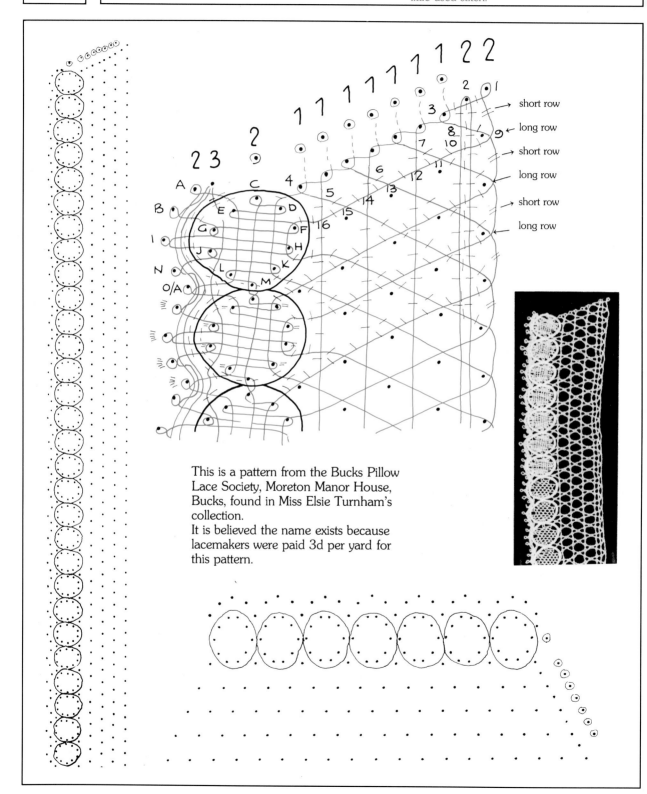

This is a pattern from the Bucks Pillow Lace Society, Moreton Manor House, Bucks, found in Miss Elsie Turnham's collection.

It is believed the name exists because lacemakers were paid 3d per yard for this pattern.

Kat stitch

Also called wire ground and French ground, kat stitch is made up of many diamonds with two vertical lines through them. All diagonal crossings have a pin under, and all vertical crossings have *no pin under*. It is made rather like honeycomb ground, with short and long rows.

> ### Kat stitch
>
> Short row – w.s., tw.1 alternate pairs from above,
> Long row – * w.s., tw.1, pin under, w.s., tw.1 *no pin*. Repeat from * to end of row.

START HERE

Hang 2 pairs in order at **1**, tw.2 both, w.s. through each other, tw.2 R.H. pair and tw.1 L.H. pair. W.s., tw.1 L.H. pair through passives at **2**, h.s., pin, h.s. through **3** to **4**. This start line 1 to 4 is only for your practice piece, it *must not* be used for serious work. This way helps you to visualise the correct positions of diagonal and vertical threads.

Short row **5**, **6** and **7** – w.s., tw.1 at **8** R.H. pair from 3 through passives, footside at 9, w.s. tw.1 and tw.2, pin under both. W.s. tw.1 L.H. pair from **9** through passives to **10**.   **11** to **16** – long row.

Whole-stitch bud

Picot (iv) at **A** (first bud only). Picot (i) at **B**. Hang 2 pairs above C, take through gimp, take gimp through 2 pairs to right and 3 pairs to left, tw.1 all 7 pairs. W.s., pin, w.s. at **C**; w.s. to **D**, tw.*2 round all pins*; 3 w.s. to **E**; 4 w.s. to **F**; *6 w.s.* to **G** (extra pair helps to keep a 'full' bud); 6 w.s. to **H**; picot (ii) at **I**; 6 w.s. to **J**; 5 w.s. to **K**; *3 w.s.* to **L**; 2 w.s. to **M**; do not cover. T.w.1 all 7 pairs coming out of bud, take gimp through and tw.1 all 7 pairs again, twist gimps right over left. Picot (iii) at **N**; 4 w.s. with pair from L; picot (ii) at **O** (new A) and 4 w.s. back. Now work is 'set in', work short and long row twice before next bud.

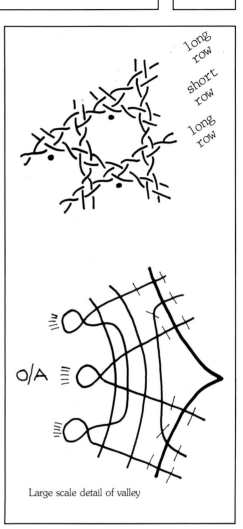

Large scale detail of valley

9 HONESTY
Bobbins 19 pairs – **Gimps** 2 pairs

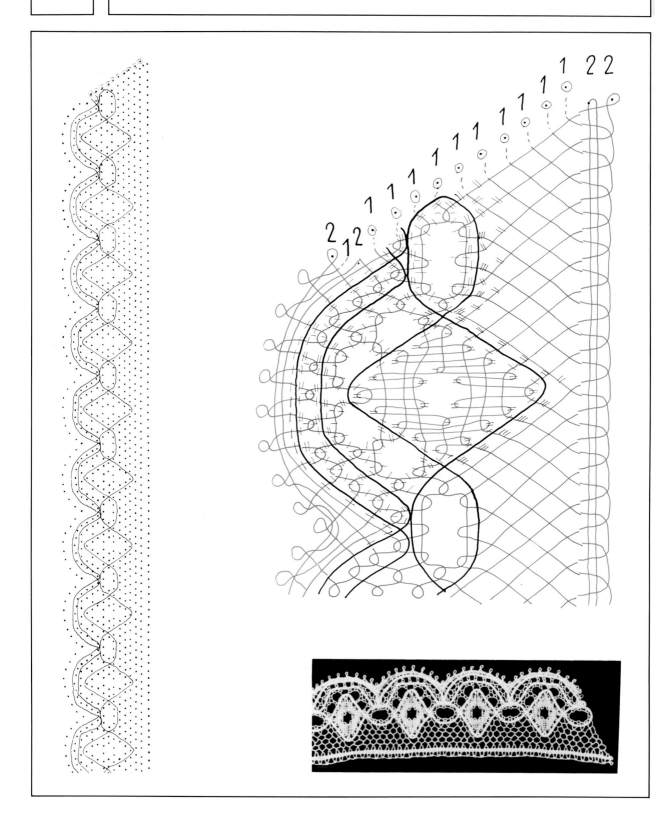

Eight-pin honeycomb ring

H.c.s. all eight pinholes – pairs hop out and work catchpin stitch on right and h.c.s. on left, twice. *Remember no twists between two adjacent gimps* (this occurs on L.H. side of ring).

Whole-stitch block with a hole

It is most important to keep all sides equal and full. Work in w.s. back and forth picking up 1 pair at end of each row, until the 2 holes level with the top middle hole have been reached. W.s. back to middle (until pair hanging down from first pinhole has been worked), pin between last two pairs, w.s. back through pairs to left and right, using two sets of workers, adding in pairs until widest part is reached, then leaving out pairs after. When workers meet at bottom pinhole: w.s., pin, w.s. L.H. pair now becomes the worker until the end of diamond, w.s. back and forth leaving out 1 pair at beginning of each row, tw.1 all 10 pairs before gimp.

How to work out your own 'holey whole-stitch'

All pairs must be equally distributed. (See also wide kat stitch pattern, page 38.)

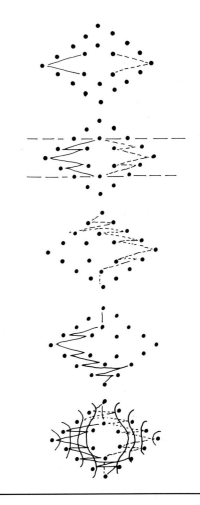

start at widest centre

in line with centre top pinhole

in line with centre bottom pinhole

right-hand worker

left-hand worker

perfect symmetry!

10 SERPENTINE

Bobbins 28 pairs – **Gimps** 4 pairs

Introducing – false picots; horizontal passives; nook pins; plaited tail

Uses – finger plate motif; sundress front panel; bookmarks

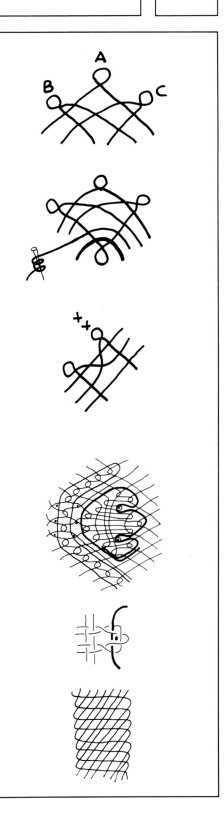

False picots – hang 2 pairs in order on pin, tw.3 both pairs, w.s. through each other, tw.1.

Top false picots

False picots at A, B and C. W.s. both pairs from B through L.H. pair from A; w.s. both pairs from C through R.H. pair from A; w.s. R.H. pair from B through 2 pairs from C; w.s. L.H. pair from C through *1 pair* from B.

Hanging on horizontal passive pairs

Wind the 2 passive pairs tightly round a pin to left of work, push the pin down into the pillow (keeps the pairs firm while using the other end), w.s. horizontal pair through L.H. pair from B and R.H. pair from C. Take gimp through these 2 pairs and quickly work first h.c.s. to keep all in place. Remove pin holding horizontal passives.

Standard false picot additions

Hang 2 pairs on each pin indicated with either 2 or + +. Work false picot on each. W.s. uppermost pair through all passives until main work; w.s. lower pair through 1 pair and leave; w.s. third pair from outside through to outer edge, work picot and return through all passives to main work.

Right-hand picots

All as L.H. picots except *pin under* R.H. thread and wind in anti-clockwise motion.

Double gimp start

Gives a good solid look top and bottom. Try to use matching pairs of gimp bobbins – this helps you to see which way each pair should go.

Three pairs of passives at footsides

Not normal practice but, as above, gives a more substantial effect.

Starting and finishing gimps in p.g.s.

Hang gimp pair on temporary pin until first stitch has been made, then let down. At end of motif, overlap gimps round at least 2 pairs each way (see diagram and note on page 41).

Nook pins

These will appear many times in the future, especially in floral work. Tw.1 worker, take through gimp, tw.2, pin under and take back through gimp and continue. In other words the workers are hooked round the gimp.

Neat finish at bottom of the piece

W.s. L.H. pair through all R.H. pairs and leave; repeat until the desired length is reached, then stop one pair before the end of each row for 4 rows. This produces a very neat plaited 'tail'. Knot in pairs and cut off to length required.

11 JOY

Bobbins 19 pairs – **Gimps** 1 pair   **Introducing** – infilled gimp weaving

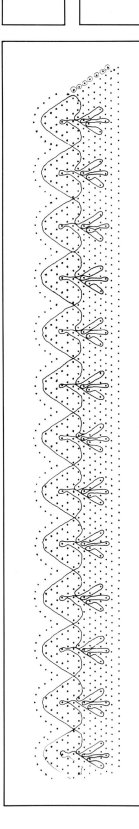

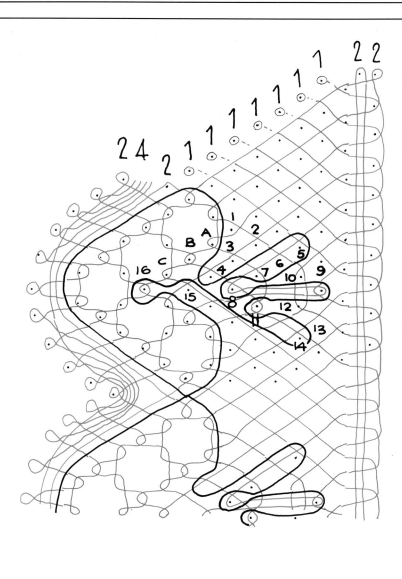

START HERE

Work as far as you can go in p.g.s., catchpin stitch and footsides. Work first long row and short row in h.c.s. and catchpin stitch at **1**. Work **A–B–C** in h.c.s. Take gimp through 2 pairs, tw.3 both. Complete p.g.s. row **2**–**3**–**4**.

Gimp 'fingers'

A very typical decoration in point ground stitch, made with only one of the gimps. Take gimp back through 6 pairs, tw.1 all 6 pairs. At **5** w.s., tw.1 R.H. pair, pin between. W.s., tw.1 R.H. pair, no pin at **6**.

Work **7** as 5. Take gimp down through 5 pairs, tw.3 first 3 pairs, tw.1 last 2 pairs. W.s., pin, w.s. last 2 pairs at **8**, tw.1 both. P.g.s. **9** and **10**; also work catchpin stitch and footsides as far as possible. Take gimp through 6 pairs to right, tw.1 all 6 pairs.

Note – w.s. R.H. pair from 8 through 4 pairs to the right, after last w.s., tw.1 R.H. pair, pin between and return in w.s. back through *5 pairs*, tw.1 all 5 pairs. Take gimp back through these 5 pairs, tw.3 first 3 pairs, tw.1 last 2 pairs. W.s., pin, w.s. at **11**; tw.1 both. Work necessary footsides and catchpin stitches and p.g.s. Pin, then p.g.s. at **12**, p.g.s. at **13**. Take gimp through 4 pairs to right; tw.2 all 4 pairs. W.s. R.H. pair from 11 through 2 pairs to right, pin under last 2 pairs at **14**; tw.1 all 3 pairs. Take gimp back and up through *9 pairs*, tw.3 first 7 pairs, tw.2 last 2 pairs. P.g.s. at **15** and h.c.s. at **16**.

Make sure the gimp is kept tight throughout this procedure

12 CONSTANCE

Bobbins 24 pairs – **Gimps** 1 pair

Introducing – starting without temporary pins; cucumber footside

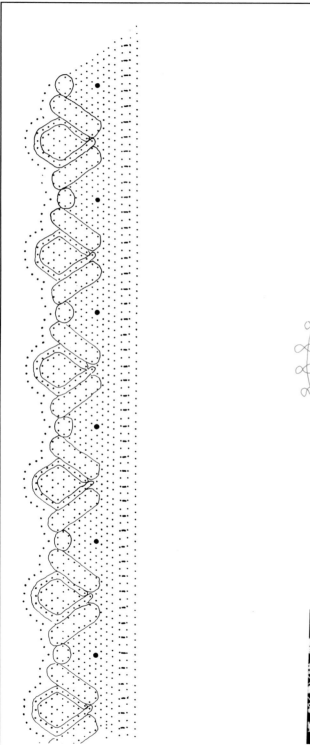

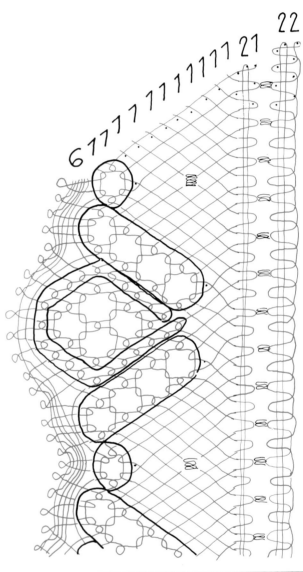

Starting without temporary pins

Put pins on start line, hang necessary pairs on each. Work your p.g.s. etc. as usual. Now for the tricky bit – remove the pin, hold the bobbins with one hand and catch the loop with the pin with other hand, then replace the pin. It takes practice but can be useful in certain instances.

Overlapping gimps

There are many overlapping gimps in this pattern – remember, *no twists* between these gimps.

Cucumber footsides

The easiest form of tally, because the two pins above keep its shape and it can be 'fixed' immediately. Remember the aim is to achieve a *wide, shallow, rectangular shape*, not square this time. Don't forget to count the number of weaves to keep them all the same size.

Another handy hint: you will note the same pair is used throughout to make the cucumber, therefore make sure there is plenty of thread on this pair!

Hang 2 pairs at **1**, tw.3 and w.s. through each other, tw.3 L.H. pair, tw.4 R.H. pair. W.s. L.H. pair through passives, tw.3 and pin under at **2**. * Return through passives and work normal footside at **3**. W.s. back through passives, tw.3 and pin under at **4***. Repeat from * to * at **5** and **6**. W.s. pair from **7** through second set of passives, work catchpin stitch at **8**, return through passives, tw.3 and pin under at **9**.

Now you are ready to make your cucumber (see notes above).

As soon as cucumber has been completed, tw.3 L.H. pair and tw.2 R.H. pair, carefully lay weaver bobbin to right of pillow and quickly w.s. the L.H. pair through L.H. passives, work next catchpin stitch, w.s. back through passives, tw.3 and pin at **10**. Return to R.H. pair from cucumber and continue as above.

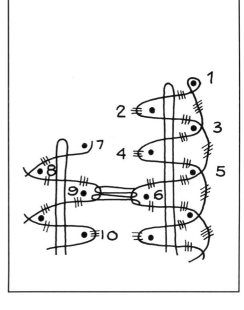

13 ROSEMARY

Bobbins 23 pairs – **Gimps** 2 pairs

Introducing – hexagonal mat; flowers; nook pins

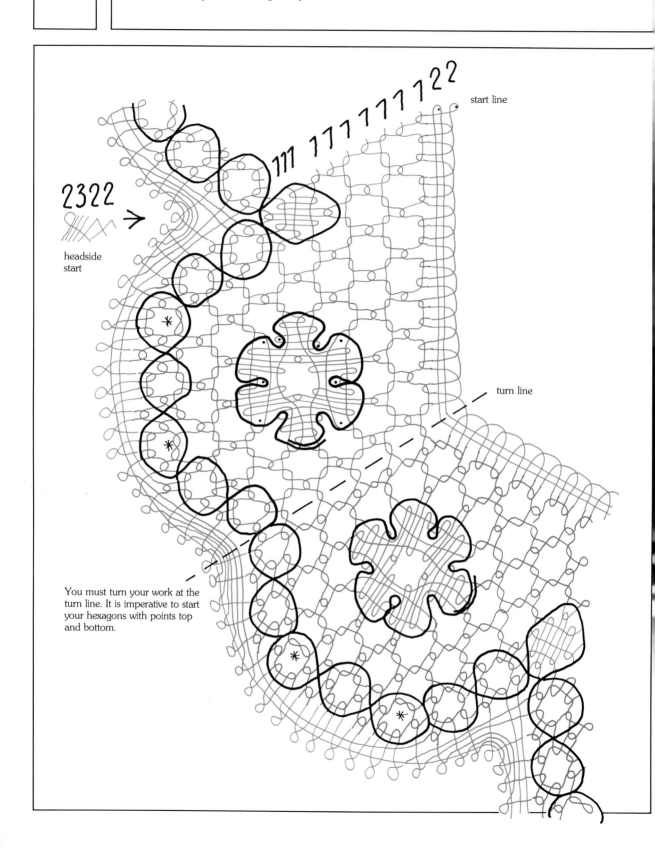

start line

2322

headside
start

turn line

You must turn your work at the
turn line. It is imperative to start
your hexagons with points top
and bottom.

Nook pin

Take worker through the gimp, tw.2 and pin, then take worker back through gimp.

START

Start on line shown on the diagram and work as usual until the flower motif.

Flower motif

Follow large scale diagram numbers, *but please note:* nook pins at 4, 5, 30 and 31. Pin between pairs only (no stitch) at 6, 7, 27 and 29. Divide workers at 10 and join again at 25. After pin 13, w.s. worker through one passive, tw.1 both, take gimp through both, tw.2 both again, pin 14, take gimp back through these pairs, tw.1 and w.s. both pairs through each other before continuing. Repeat this also after pin 20 and pin 21. Overlap gimps at end – take both gimps through 4 pairs, throw back and cut off as on page 41.

* pinchain stitch here (h.c.s., pin, h.c.s., pin, h.c.s.).

Do take care at the *turn line*. So many beginners forget to turn their pillow, carry on downwards and then find too many bobbins one edge and not enough the other! After the turn line h.c.s. have been made, the rows *must* be made in the opposite direction – e.g. from headside to footside – until that 'corner' is turned.

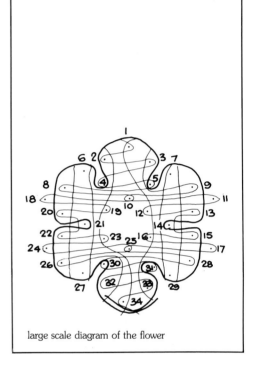

large scale diagram of the flower

← start line

14 WAVES
Bobbins 21 pairs + 2 short-length pairs – **Gimps** 2 pairs

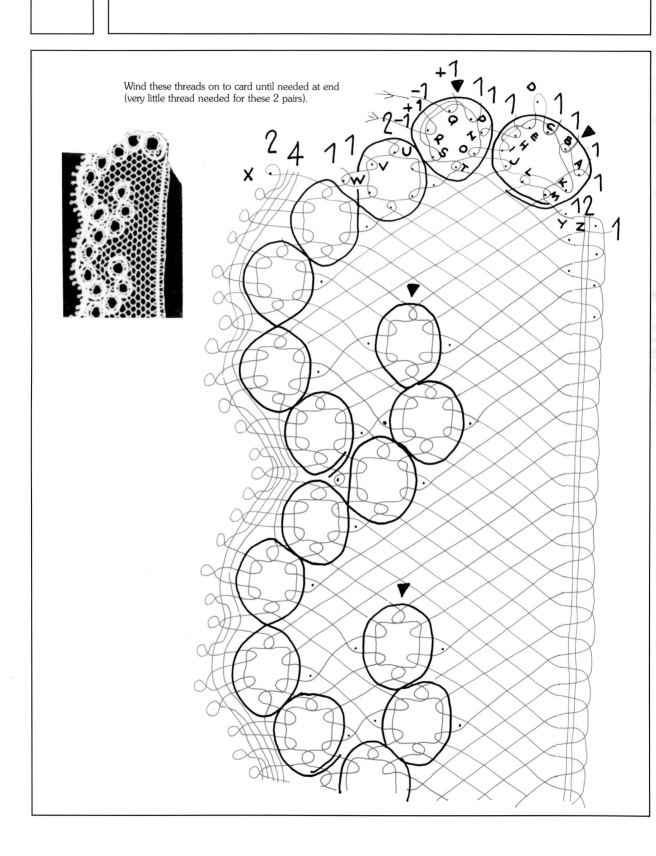

Wind these threads on to card until needed at end
(very little thread needed for these 2 pairs).

Start line

Hopefully this will give the best invisible join at the end, which is our aim in Bucks Point lace.)

Hang gimps above A and N. Hang on 1 pair above B, C, H, N, P, Q, R, U, V, W and Y. Hang 2 pairs above A, U and passives Z. Take all these pairs through gimp and tw.2.

H.c.s. **A**, **B** and **C**, take L.H. pair from C through gimp, tw.2 round pin at **D** (ready now for sewing at end), take this pair back through gimp. H.c.s. **E** with pair from above. H.c.s. through 2 pairs from E, pin **H** between 2 inside pairs and h.c.s. back through 2 pairs, take through gimp. H.c.s. **I**, take L.H. pair through gimp and new gimp when available (remember no twists between 2 gimps). H.c.s. **N** with a new pair and pair from H; h.c.s. **O** with pairs from N and I; h.c.s. **P** with a new pair and pair from N; h.c.s. **J** with pairs from I and O; h.c.s. **K** with pairs from B and A; h.c.s. **L** with pairs from J and K; h.c.s. **M** with pairs from L and K.

Take gimp through the bottom pairs of this ring, overlap and throw back as note on page 41. H.c.s. pair from above Q through 2 pairs from P, pin **Q** between 2 inside pairs. H.c.s. back through 2 pairs, take through gimp, tw.3 (leave these threads wound on to card until the end, when they will be rewound on bobbins to make a neat end). With pair above R, work **R** as Q; with 2 pairs from R, h.c.s. **S**; h.c.s. **T** with pairs from S and O; take gimp round, cross over and through 2 pairs above U and new pair above J; work normal h.c.s. ring starting at **U**. Hang 2 pairs at **X**, tw.5 and w.s. through each other, tw.1, hang 4 pairs on pin as on page 40.

Footside start

P.g.s. pair from M with new pair at **Y**. W.s. through 2 passive pairs at **Z**, tw.3, w.s. through pair at footside, pin under both.

Now all is set for a normal working until next corner.

14A WAVES CORNER
Bobbins 4 extra pairs – **Gimps** 1 extra pair

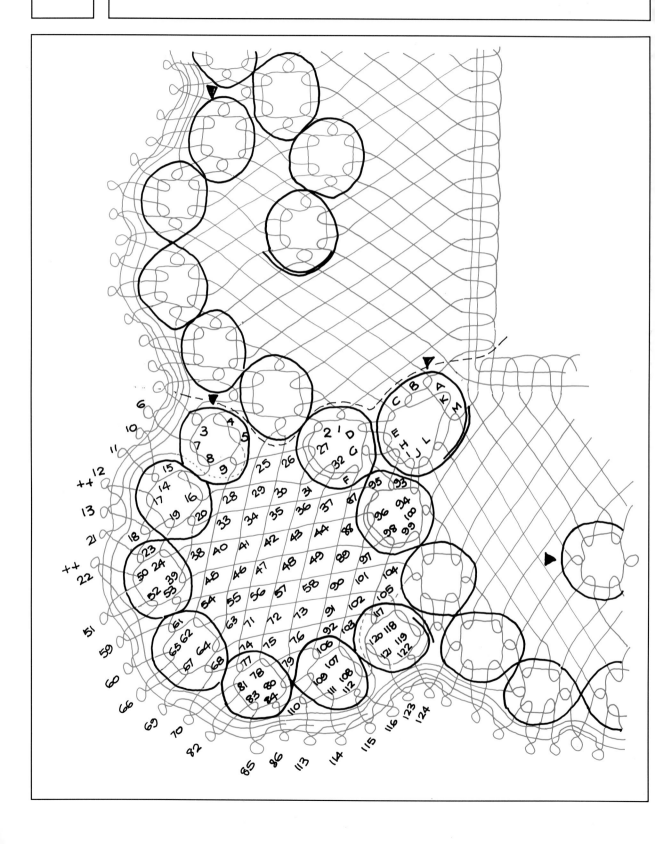

Work as usual until dotted line. Hang third gimp above A, h.c.s. **A**, **B** and **C**. H.c.s **1** and **2**, take L.H. pair from C through 2 gimps, h.c.s. **D** back through gimps, h.c.s. **E**. Hang new gimp above 3, h.c.s. **3**, pinchain **4** and **5** (h.s., tw.1, pin, h.s., tw.1, pin h.s., tw.1), picot (i) **6**, pinchain **7** and **8** h.c.s. **9**. Note: there is nowhere for R.H. pair from 5 to go, so it is taken round with the gimp until it becomes one of the heading passives (dotted line).

Picot (i) **10** and **11**, false picot (see page 25) at **12**. Picot (i) **13**, h.c.s. **14**, pinchain **15** and **16**. H.c.s. **17**, **18**, **19** and **20**. Picot (i) **21**, false picot **22**, h.c.s. **23** and **24**. P.g.s. **25** and **26**, h.s., tw.1, h.s., tw.1, pin **27** between 2 R.H. pairs, h.s., tw.1, h.s., tw.1, back. P.g.s. **28**, **29**, **30**, catchpin stitch **31**, work **32** as 27, h.c.s. **F** and **G**. P.g.s. **33** to **37**, catchpin stitch **38**, h.c.s. **39**, p.g.s. **40** to **44** and **45** to **49**. H.c.s. **50**, picot (ii) **51**, h.c.s. **52** and **53**, p.g.s. **54** to **58**, picot (ii) **59**. Picot (i) **60**, h.c.s. **61** and **62**, catchpin stitch **63**, h.c.s. **64** and **65**. Picot (ii) **66**, h.c.s. **67** and **68**, picot (iii) **69**, picot (ii) **70**. P.g.s. **71** to **73** and **74** to **76**. H.c.s **77** and **78**, catchpin stitch **79**. H.c.s **80** and **81**, picot (ii) **82**. H.c.s. **83** and **84**, picot (iii) **85** and **86**.

After 86 has been completed, throw 1 pair out, also after 113, 114 and 115. P.g.s. **87** to **92**. With R.H. pair from G, take through 2 pairs gimp, work **H** as 27, h.c.s. **I**. H.c.s. **93** to **96** as 27, catchpin stitch **97** and **98** as 27, h.c.s. **99** and **100**. P.g.s. **101** to **105**, h.c.s. **106** to **108** as 4 and 5 above, h.c.s. **109** to **112**. Picot (iii) **113** to **116**, take pair from passives round with gimp until needed at 125, h.c.s. **117** to **119** and **120** and **121** as 4 and 5 above. H.c.s. **122**, picot (iii) **123**, picot (ii) **124**. H.c.s. **J**, **K**, **L** and **M**.

W.s. pair from last footside catchpin worked, through inner footside passive – they in effect now change places. Old inside passive now ready to work catchpin stitch with R.H. pair from M then back through passive pairs; w.s. with outer pair; pin under both.

Now you are ready to proceed as normal.

15 AIDA

Bobbins 32 pairs – **Gimps** 1 pair + 1 single

Introducing – other ways of working headings; whole-stitch blocks; fingers; eight-pin honeycomb rings

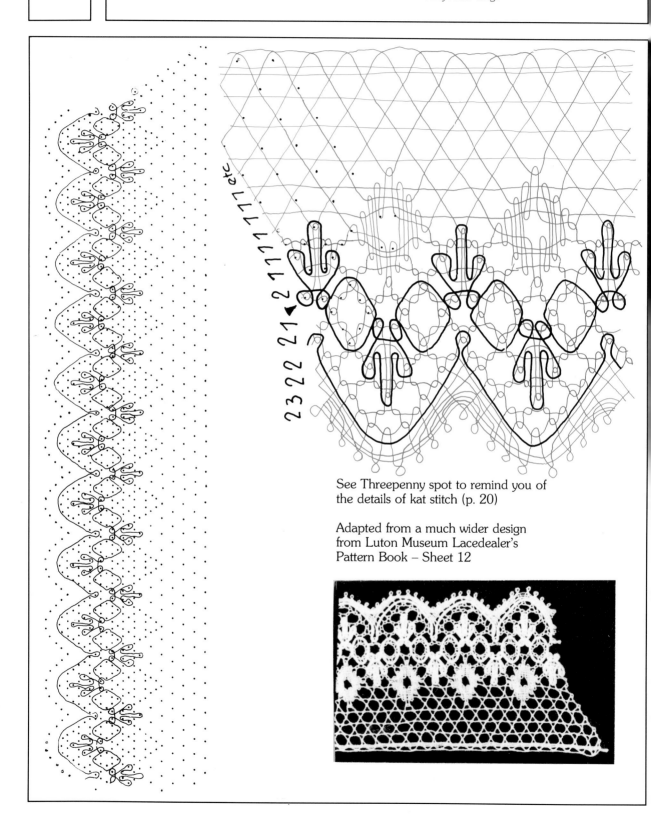

1 1 1 1 1 1 1 2 etc

2 1 22 23

See Threepenny spot to remind you of the details of kat stitch (p. 20)

Adapted from a much wider design from Luton Museum Lacedealer's Pattern Book – Sheet 12

Different heading method

Use *third pair* instead of second pair from outer edge to make picot and, in reverse, take picot pair back through *2 pairs* and leave.

Gimp fingers, type II

W.s. inside gimp 'fingers' throughout. T.w.1 before and after gimp, except tw.2 at nook pin.

Eight-pin honeycomb ring

Take gimp through 3 pairs each side, tw.2, h.c.s. top 3 pinholes A, B and D. h.s., tw.1 pair from C through 2 pairs from B, pin between 2 L.H. pairs. h.s., tw.1 pair to left of pin through 2 pairs to right pin between 2 R.H. pairs (E). H.s., tw.1. these 2 R.H. pairs. Repeat in reverse at F and G. Honeycomb stitch at bottom pinhole as usual.

Whole-stitch block with four-pin hole

W.s. back and forth picking up one pair each side until*. At *, w.s. to left through 3 pairs, return picking up last pair at end. W.s. to left through 4 pairs, pin under, *leave*. Pin between last 2 R.H. pairs of L.H. side. W.S. pair to right of pin to left through 4 pairs, pin, w.s. back to centre pin. Now w.s. back and forth leaving pairs out at each pinhole as usual. T.w.2 all 10 pairs.

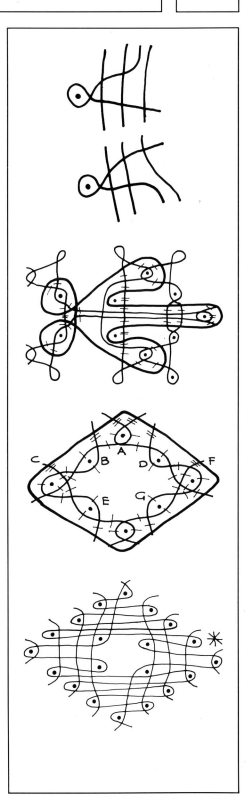

16 SEA URCHIN

Bobbins 25 pairs – **Gimps** 3 pairs

Introducing – circular lace; hanging on a pin; four-pin buds

Can be used as a pretty motif decorating a patch pocket, also as a small sampler.

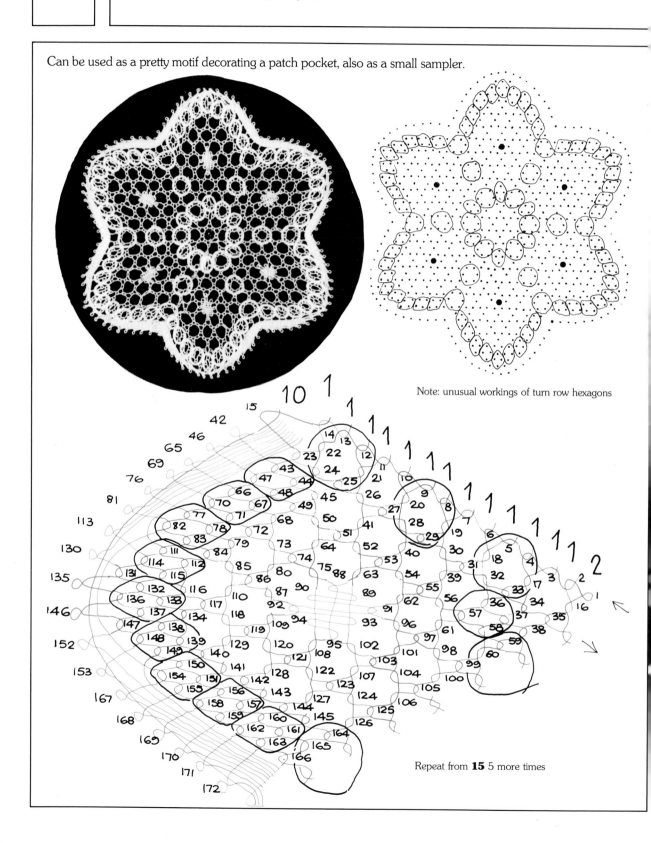

Note: unusual workings of turn row hexagons

Repeat from **15** 5 more times

Multiple hanging on a pin

Whenever there are so many passive pairs at a valley start, this is a good method to use: hang the required number of pairs in pairs carefully on one pin. After valley pin and first pin inside the valley pin have been worked, *carefully* lay passive pin sideways (supported on the two other pins).

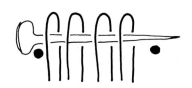

Four-pin honeycomb buds

Honeycomb in this order. When honeycomb hops out of gimp it sometimes helps to make *w.s.*, tw.1, pin, h.s., tw.1, to keep its shape (see nos 23, 131, 147 and 166.)

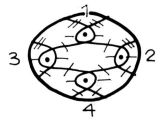

Finishing off gimps

Complete honeycomb ring. Take R.H. gimp through 3 pairs to left, and L.H. gimp 3 pairs to right (you will see gimps overlap). Throw gimps back until work has progressed considerably – usually until gimps are next needed! Cut off, leaving 5 cm (2 in.) ends. Use curved nail scissors to cut close to work when clear of pins.

   It really makes life easier if you use heavy gimp bobbins for this pattern. I like to use matching brass bobbins. It is so important to keep the gimp tight round the pins.

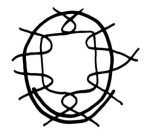

Working a circular motif

There are basically two methods of working a circular motif: this is the easiest. Made in six sections on 60° graph. *This circle keeps better shape and requires fewer bobbins.* Work one triangular section, then move whole pillow 60° and start again.

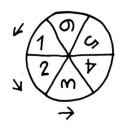

START HERE

Work entirely in h.c.s. except, of course, the headside and mayflowers. Start with 2 pairs at **1**. Take good note of unusual workings at 111 and 154; this helps fill in that awkward space.

17 MURIEL

Bobbins 38 pairs – **Gimps** 6 pairs + 2 single gimps

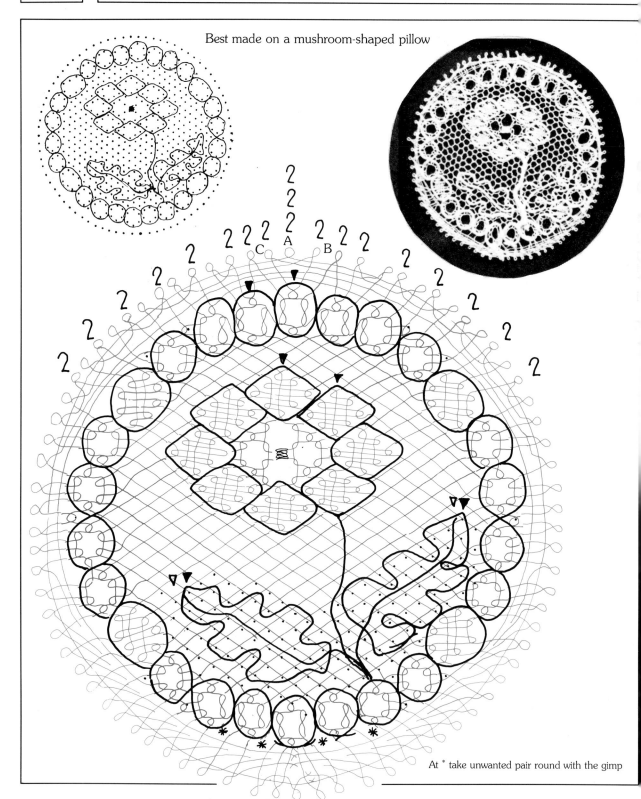

Best made on a mushroom-shaped pillow

2
2
2
2
2 2 2 2 2 2 2
C A B
2
2
2
2
2
2
2
2
2

D E F

At * take unwanted pair round with the gimp

False picots

Hang 2 pairs in order on a pin, tw.3 both, w.s. through each other and tw.1 both.

False picots after introductory picots

After picot has been made, w.s. uppermost pair through passives and gimp, then use in main work. W.s. second pair from picot through 2 pairs and leave. Then w.s. third pair from outside edge through to next picot. Work normal picot then w.s. through to main work area. (See page 25 for diagrams to refresh your memory.)

Right-hand picot

All as L.H. picot, except *pin under* R.H. thread and wind in anti-clockwise motion.

Pinchain

H.c.s., pin, h.c.s., pin, h.c.s.

START HERE

Make false picots on top 7 pinholes. Take L.H. pair from top centre pinhole through all 6 pairs to left. Take R.H. pair from top centre pinhole through all 6 pairs to right. Take L.H. pair from B through all 6 pairs to left. Take R.H. pair from C through all *5 pairs* to right. Hang 4 pairs horizontally and take them through all eight pairs.

Top and bottom five rings

These have pinchain stitch in them; this enables the gimps to flow easily.

Leaves

These are achieved by just weaving the gimps round in p.g.s. Just follow the lines on the pricking. One handy hint: work the two rows p.g.s. below L.H. side of flower, then all the R.H. leaf can be made. N.B. When not working complete rows of p.g.s. always remember p.g.s. is a series of diamonds on their sides and only when the top three pinholes have been worked can the last bottom stitch be worked. *Threads never travel vertically in p.g.s.*

This method of working a circle has one very great point in its favour: the threads are *thrown out* as your work progresses, so there are not thousands of pairs to be sewn off at the end!

Throwing out pairs

When there are more than 3 pairs in the edge passives during the second half of the motif, throw out the second pair from the gimp.

At the end

At D, w.s. through 4 pairs, picot and back through 4 pairs, throw back. Turn pillow 45°, work second pair from outside edge, w.s. to outside, make picot E and w.s. back through 1 pair. Straighten pillow again, w.s. through 4 pairs, picot F and back through 2 pairs, tie off the 2 passive pairs with adjacent pairs, continue w.s. through last 2 pairs then throw back and tie off last 2 passive pairs. Sew in the 2 pairs thrown back with a needle round gimps.

18 OLNEY HANDKERCHIEF

Bobbins 49 pairs – **Gimps** 2 pairs

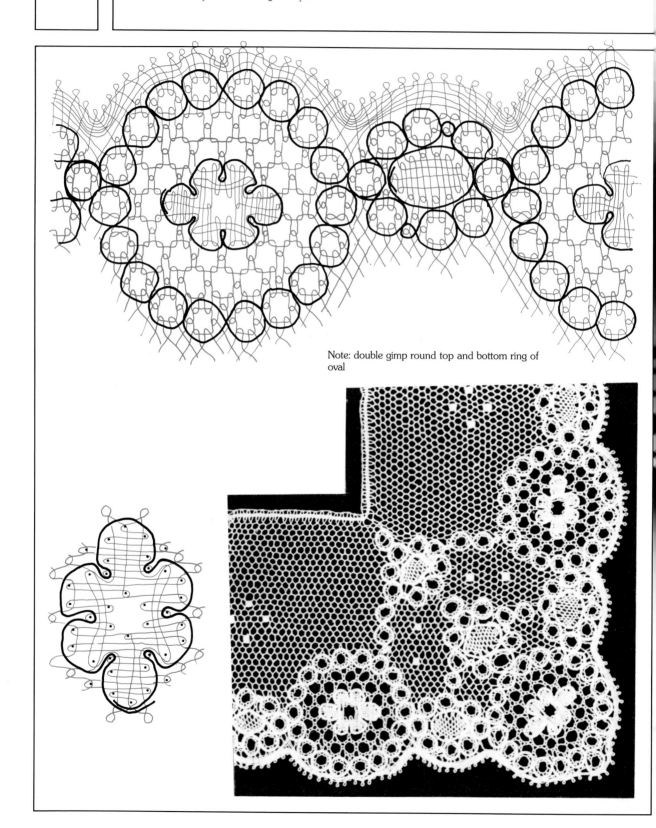

Note: double gimp round top and bottom ring of
oval

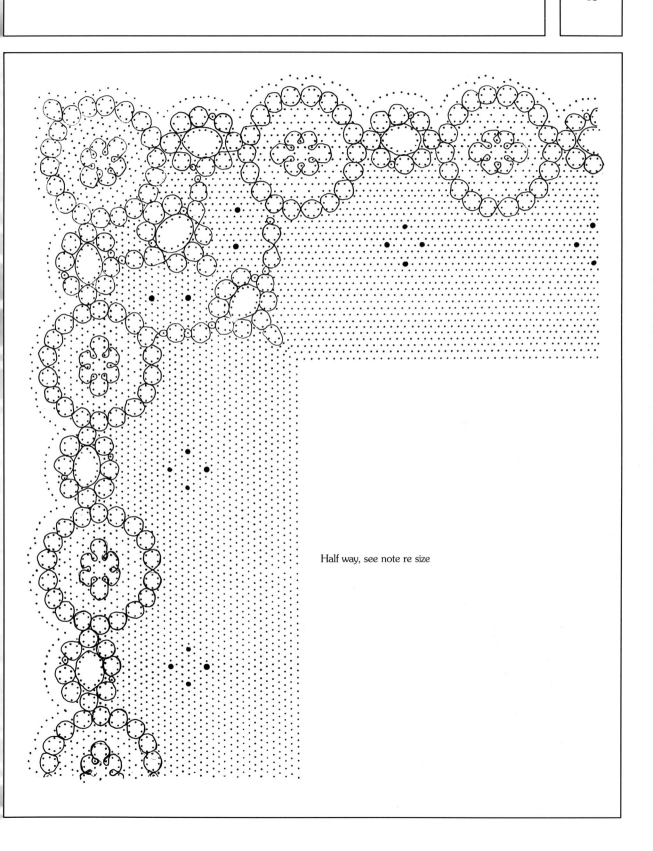

Half way, see note re size

18A OLNEY HANDKERCHIEF CORNER

Bobbins 49 pairs + approx. 16 pairs – **Gimps** 2 pairs + approx. 7 for corners

Note: gimp finishes shown below are diagramatic –
gimps *must* overlap at least 2 stitches each way

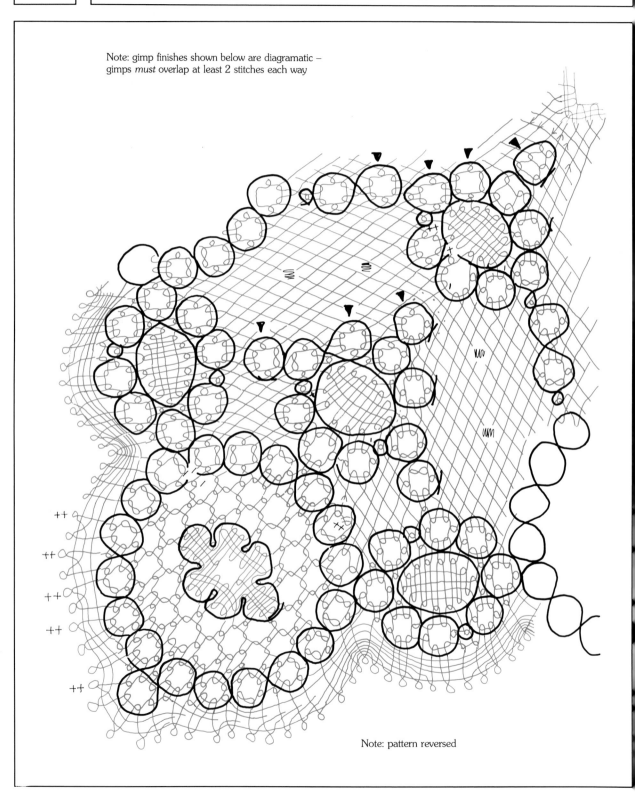

Note: pattern reversed

Footside corner note

This is a very neat version; you do not have to go round the corner pin three times as usual. Work footside as normal until catchpin A has been worked. W.s. R.H. pair from A through the 2 passives, leave. W.s. the 2 passives through each other, leave. L.H. pair from last stitch can now work 2 p.g.s. After corner has been turned and the 3 rings nearest the footside have been completed, work 2 p.g.s. from nearest ring, w.s. R.H. pair through 2 pairs to its right (temporary passives), leave. W.s. 2 pairs temporary passives through each other, tw.3 L.H. pair, pin under and leave. P.g.s. next row down from B. Catchpin stitch with pair waiting on a pin.

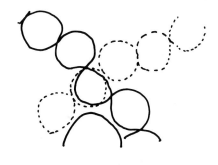

Double gimps at top and bottom of oval sections: try to use matching pairs of gimp bobbins; this helps you to see which way each pair goes.

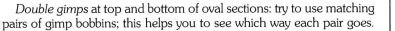

General notes

Internal catchpin stitches every time outside honeycomb rings are next to net. I have tried to copy the original as exactly as possible except when I felt a better solution could be found. You will notice there are many figures of eight (pin-chain stitches h.s., tw.1, pin, h.s., tw.1, pin, h.s., tw.1) used to help the flow of gimps.

The original handkerchief has one more repeat than shown, which makes a very large hanky – 34 cm ($13\frac{1}{2}$ in.) square – even the material centre is 21 cm ($8\frac{1}{4}$ in.) square! This version makes a 26.5 cm ($10\frac{1}{2}$ in.) square hanky overall, which is surely enough?

USES FOR LACE STRIPS

Don't just make lace – use it and wear it

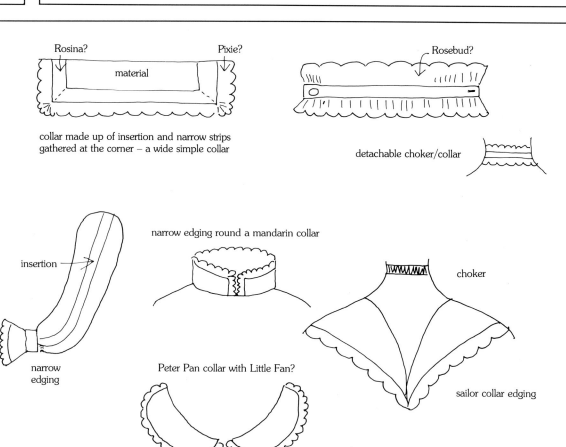

Rosina?   Pixie?

material

collar made up of insertion and narrow strips
gathered at the corner – a wide simple collar

Rosebud?

detachable choker/collar

insertion

narrow edging round a mandarin collar

choker

narrow
edging

Peter Pan collar with Little Fan?

sailor collar edging

Serpentine/Rosina/Saffron – elongate these and add tails both ends to
make a very interesting choker, epecially when made in silk; backed on to
ribbon and elastic they would make a headband for a little bridesmaid;
behind perspex to make fingerplates for your doors and, of course, a first
class present as bookmarks.

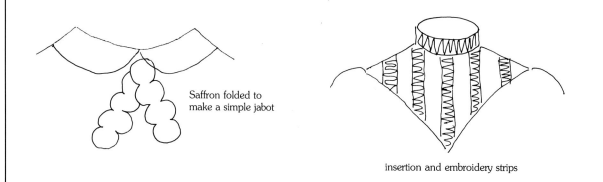

Saffron folded to
make a simple jabot

insertion and embroidery strips

I hope that by now you have learnt enough to follow the prickings and diagrams, and will not need so many words. (Remember, in the old days, lacemakers only had the pricking to interpret as they thought best!) But I shall continue to explain the complicated sections.

The following are a few handy hints which I have found useful over the years, and which I would like to pass on to you.

1. **Plan ahead** – a good slogan to apply to all your lacework; think out the order of working to avoid moving bobbins back and forth unnecessarily which is unproductive and also increases the chance of them getting in a muddle.

2. When moving a **batch of bobbins**, use the flat of the hand – this reduces the possibility of the bobbins hopping over each other.

3. Work **just enough ground**, so that you can work a whole pattern, before moving the net bobbins again.

4. **Watch your work**, not your bobbins, so hopefully you will see mistakes almost before they happen! Also, if you do look down at the bobbins all the time, you will end up with 'lacemakers neckache' (very painful).

5. **Correct and Comfortable Posture Essential**.

6. Make a habit of frequently **stroking your bobbins gently downwards**. I cannot stress enough the importance of this; in fine threadwork, a good old Torchon tug would be disastrous.

7. Hold the passive bobbins with the flat of one hand as you pull the worker up after a long line of whole stitch or half stitch.

8. To help your speed, **look ahead, and search out the next pin** to be extracted (e.g. while twisting in point ground and especially during headpin twist 5).

9. Another way to work **p.g.s** – work a whole row of diagonal stitches *then pin up*. This looks quick but I have my doubts; also you must be very accurate with your pinning. Apparently the very experienced lacemakers used no pins!

10. **When lost in p.g.s.** always look for your diamond on its side; if the top three stitches have been worked, it is safe to work number 4.

11. Remember there is always 1 pair **between pins** in net, but 2 pairs between catchpin and first pin to its left.

12. Threads in p.g.s. never travel horizontally or vertically; also remember **you can never work uphill**.

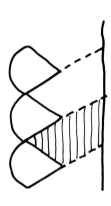

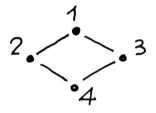

19 CANDIDA

Bobbins 20 pairs – **Gimps** 1 pair

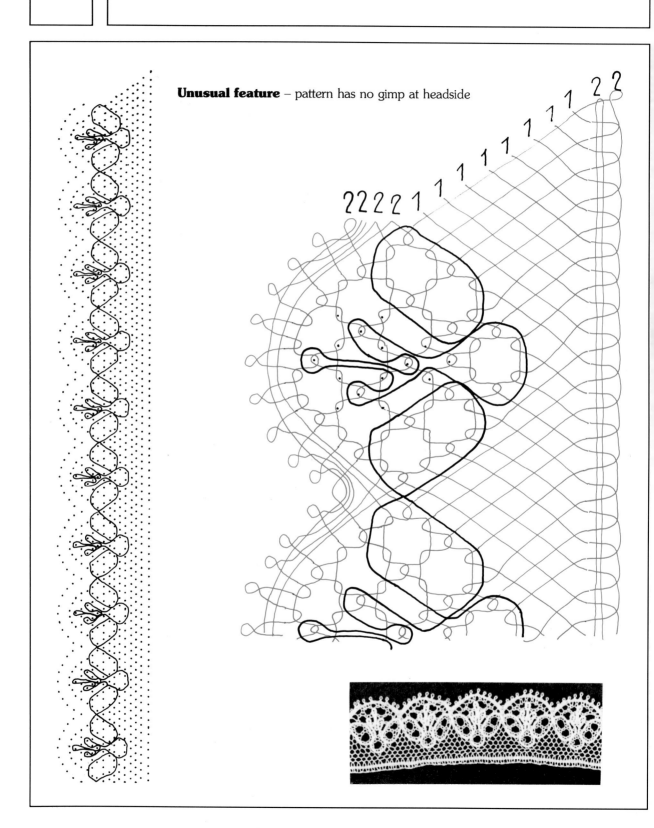

Unusual feature – pattern has no gimp at headside

2 2 2 2 1 1 1 1 1 1 1 1 1 1 2 2

20 SAFFRON

Bobbins 24 pairs – **Gimps** 1 pair

Introducing – fingers in point ground; increasings and decreasings in work, not headsides

51

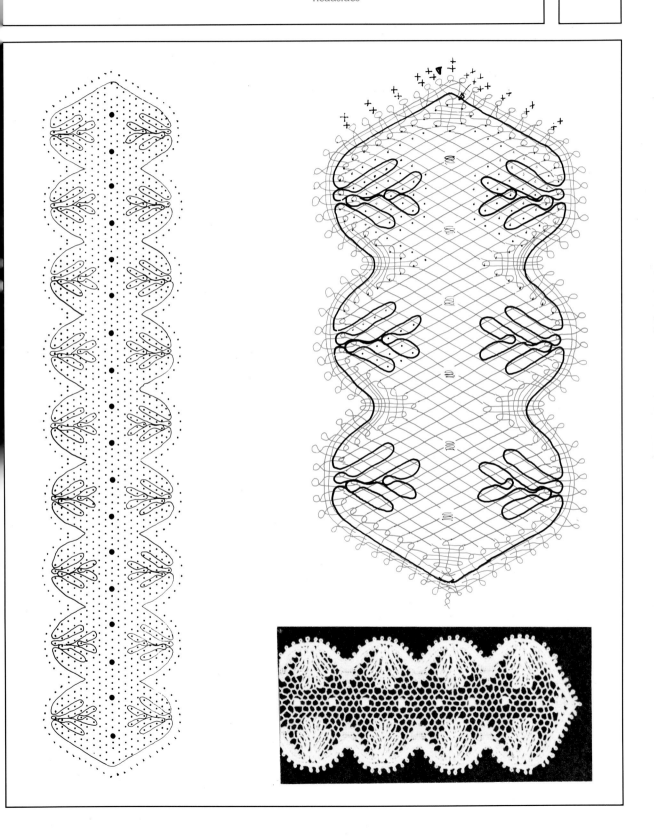

21 PAPILLON

Bobbins 22 pairs – **Gimps** 2 pairs

Introducing – footside start; double zigzags

Suitable for pill box lids

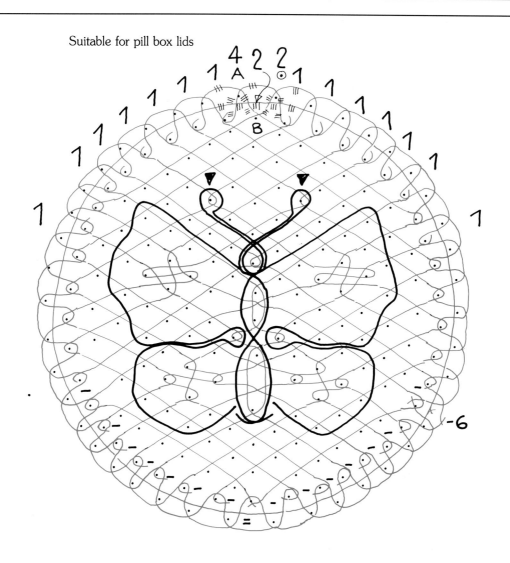

Brok 80

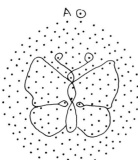

A ⊙

Brok 140 pill box size

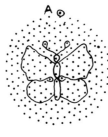

A ⊙

Note: I have moved the bottom finishing off round to the right (fewer knots in one place here)

FOOTSIDE START

Start at A with 4 pairs *in order*, w.s. 2 L.H. pairs, tw.3 all 4 pairs. W.s. R.H. pair from A through L.H. pair from temporary pin. Pin between these 2 pairs, remove temporary pin, tw.3 all three pairs.

Hanging on horizontal passive pairs

Wind the 2 passive pairs tightly round a pin to left of work, push the pin down into the pillow (keeps the pairs firm while using the other end), w.s. and tw.3 R.H. pair from pin through 4 middle pairs. T.w.3 all vertical pairs. P.g.s. and pin at B with centre 2 pairs.

Hanging on single pairs internally

Hang new pair on the pin. W.s. pair hanging to right of B through this new pair. T.w.3 both and return to normal footside edging. The new pair is now ready to work the ground.

Double zigzag four-pin bud

Gives a much fuller effect than the normal four-pin bud (see bottom half of wings for usual four-pin bud). W.s. and pin between pairs at W. W.s. pair from X through 3 pairs to right. Pin and return through these 3 pairs, pin at Y and w.s. back through 3 pairs; leave. Put in pin Z and w.s. 2 R.H. pairs below it. T.w.3 all 4 pairs.

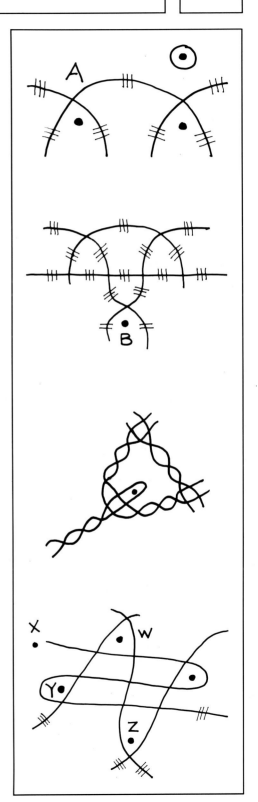

22 MARIANNE
Bobbins 22 pairs – **Gimps** 2 pairs

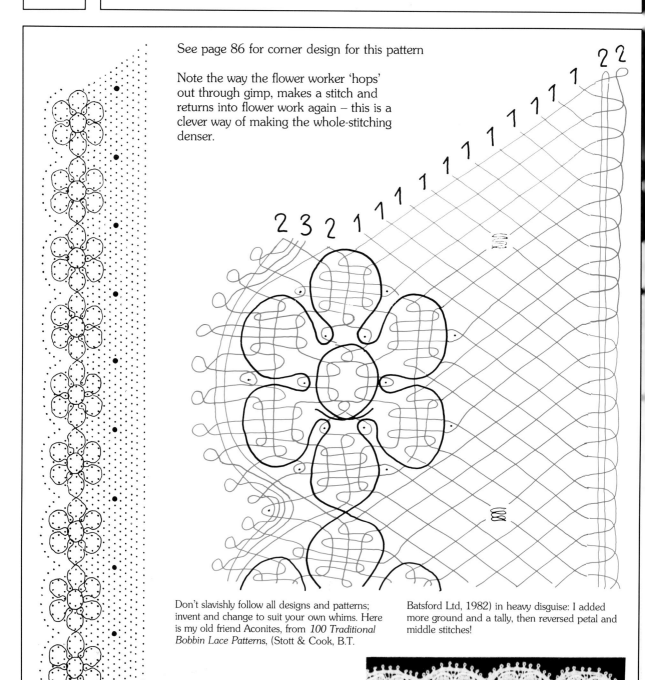

See page 86 for corner design for this pattern

Note the way the flower worker 'hops' out through gimp, makes a stitch and returns into flower work again – this is a clever way of making the whole-stitching denser.

Don't slavishly follow all designs and patterns; invent and change to suit your own whims. Here is my old friend Aconites, from *100 Traditional Bobbin Lace Patterns*, (Stott & Cook, B.T. Batsford Ltd, 1982) in heavy disguise: I added more ground and a tally, then reversed petal and middle stitches!

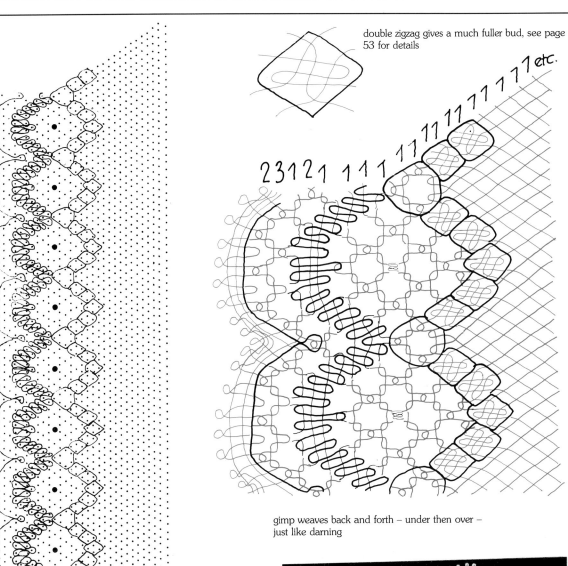

double zigzag gives a much fuller bud, see page 53 for details

2 3 1 2 1   1 1 1 1   1 1 1 1 1 1 1 1 etc.

gimp weaves back and forth – under then over – just like darning

24 ROSEBUD
Bobbins 12 pairs – **Gimps** 1 single

Christening set – narrow border (for neckline and sleeves?)

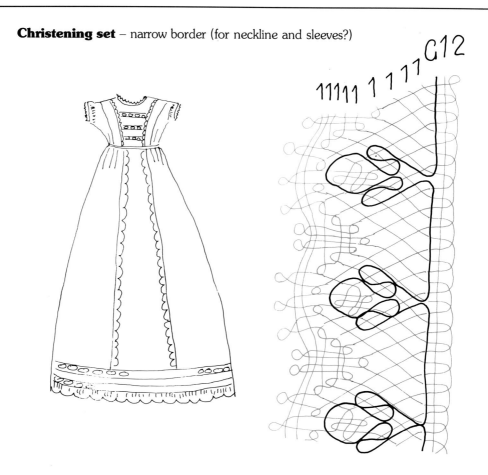

The first four-pin bud in sample has been constructed in the usual zigzag way, but the rest have been constructed in the 'double zigzag' method; this clearly shows how much fuller and better the double method looks.

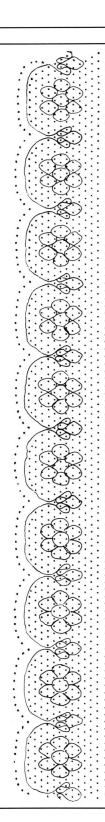

Christening set – medium border (bottom of dress?)

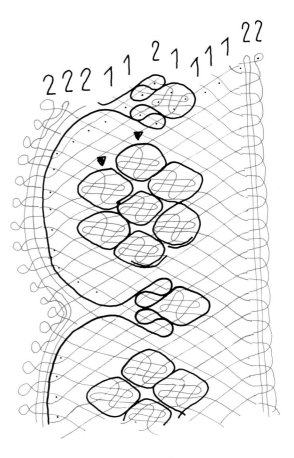

Keeping the theme of Rosebud and adding a small dainty half-stitch flower, make this neat border for your matching set. To achieve a better shape for the flower I have used a 60° graph (instead of the usual 56°) for all these Christening patterns.

26 CINDERELLA

Bobbins 48 pairs – **Gimps** 16 pairs

Christening set – bonnet back

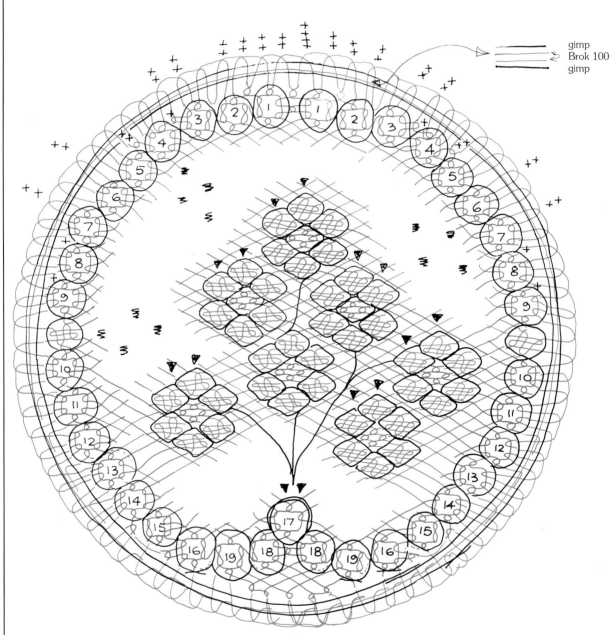

gimp
Brok 100
gimp

take redundant threads round with gimps whenever possible

honeycomb ring gimps end at bottom of rings 16 and 19 (both sides)

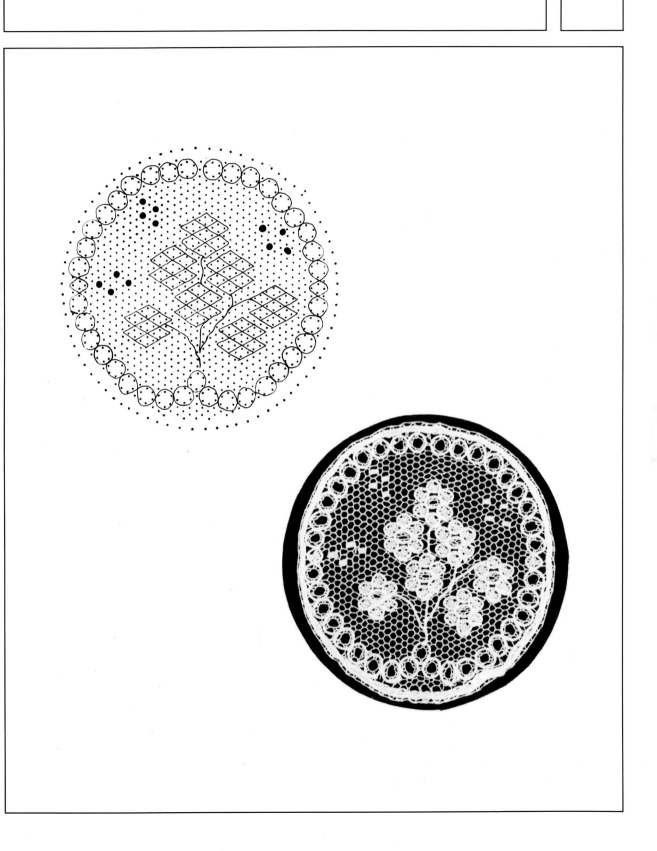

27 ROSINA

Bobbins 18 pairs – **Gimps** 2 single + 2 pairs

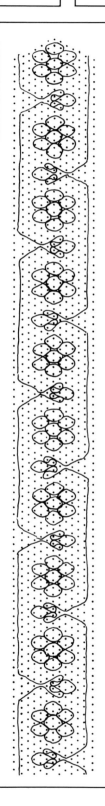

Christening set – insertion

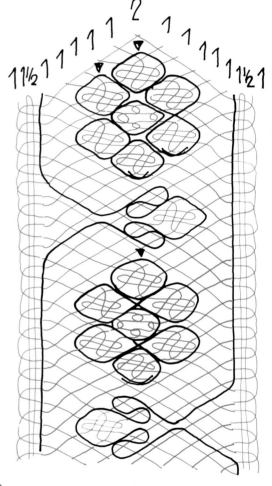

either

or

Had a problem at footside:
1 pair passives + gimp was too thin;
2 pairs passives + gimp was too thick.
So, half-way down the sample, I have
added a single thread and worked it
with the gimp as its pair. At the 3 holes
when gimp disappears, work first two
threads as one.

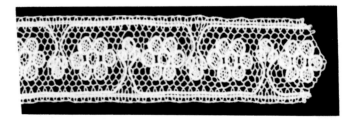

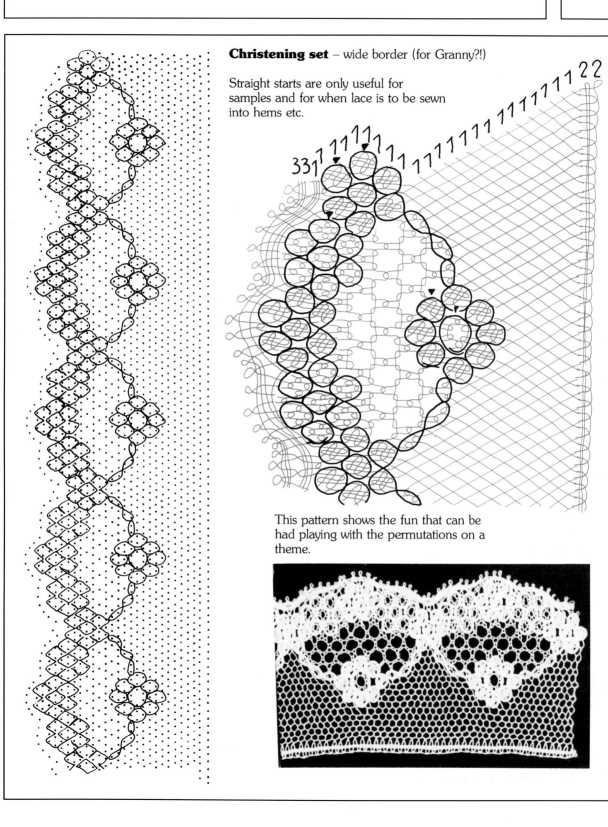

Christening set – wide border (for Granny?!)

Straight starts are only useful for samples and for when lace is to be sewn into hems etc.

33

This pattern shows the fun that can be had playing with the permutations on a theme.

29 LINDA
Bobbins 36 pairs – **Gimps** 3 pairs + 4 pairs for corner

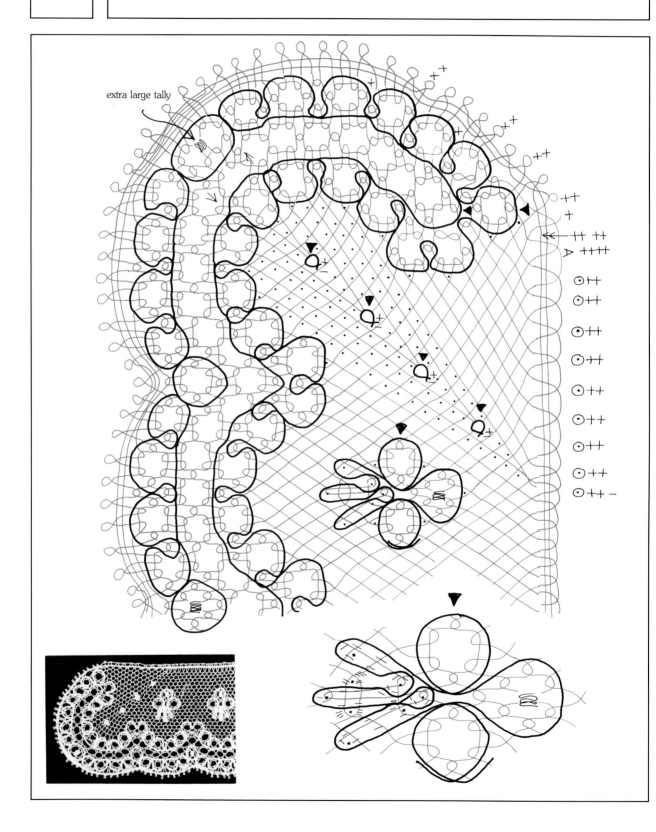

extra large tally

Measure length of collar required first. Please do not make your lace and then find it will fit nothing, as one poor friend of mine did!

FOOTSIDE START

Start at A with 4 pairs *in order*, w.s. 2 L.H. pairs, tw.3 all 4 pairs. W.s. R.H. pair from A through L.H. pair from temporary pin. Pin between these 2 pairs. Remove temporary pin, tw.3 all 3 pairs.

Hanging on horizontal passive pairs

Wind the 4 passive pairs tightly round a pin to left of work, push the pin down into the pillow (this keeps the pairs firm while using the other end). W.s. 2 R.H. pairs through all vertical pairs, tw.3 all vertical pairs. Pin then p.g.s. vertical pairs as shown on diagram. Add only one pair to left of A, the other additions are either false picots or hanging over gimps at start of h.c. rings.

Unusual adding-in within p.g.s

Needed to keep the desired design. I have used small gimp circles to disguise this join. Take gimp through existing pair, tw.1. Hang new pair on the pin, w.s. through existing pair. T.w.1 both, take through gimp, tw.3, then normal p.g.s. *up* to rings. When the p.g.s. returns, take it through gimp, tw.1. W.s. through existing pair, round pin and through gimp the other side, tw.1 existing pair, overlap both gimps through these 2 pairs. Tie a reef knot in both pairs (gimps inclined to unravel if not knotted). Throw back pair no longer needed and, later, neatly sew these threads round gimp ring.

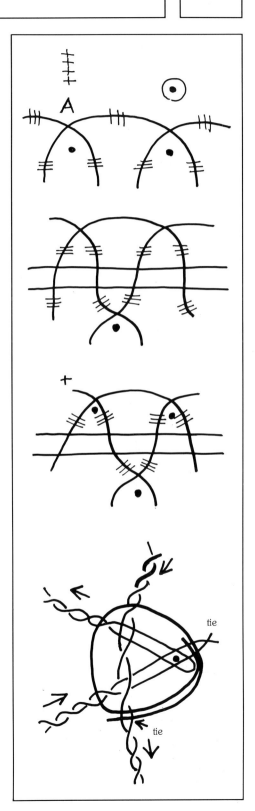

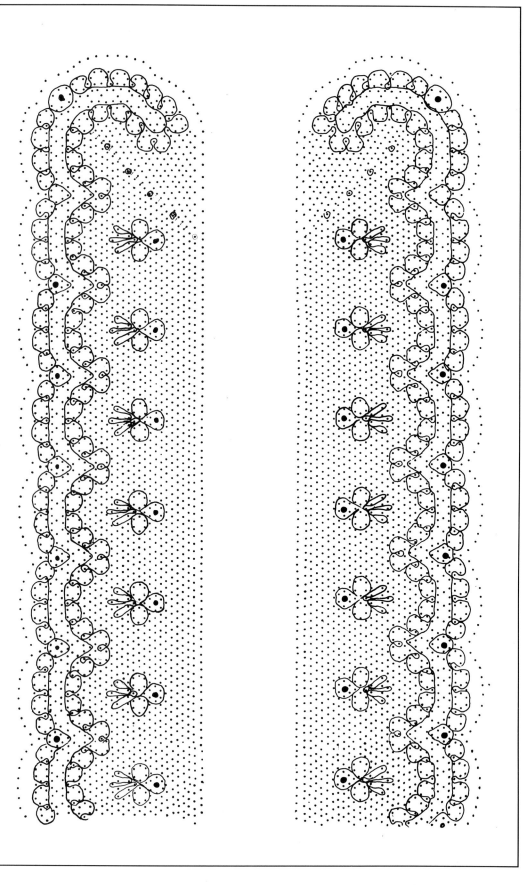

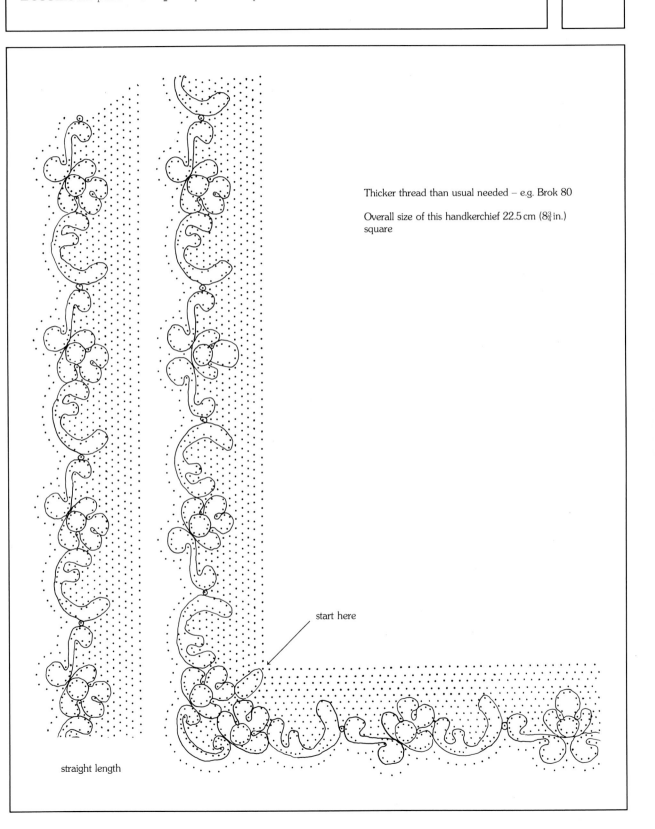

Thicker thread than usual needed – e.g. Brok 80

Overall size of this handkerchief 22.5 cm (8¾ in.) square

start here

straight length

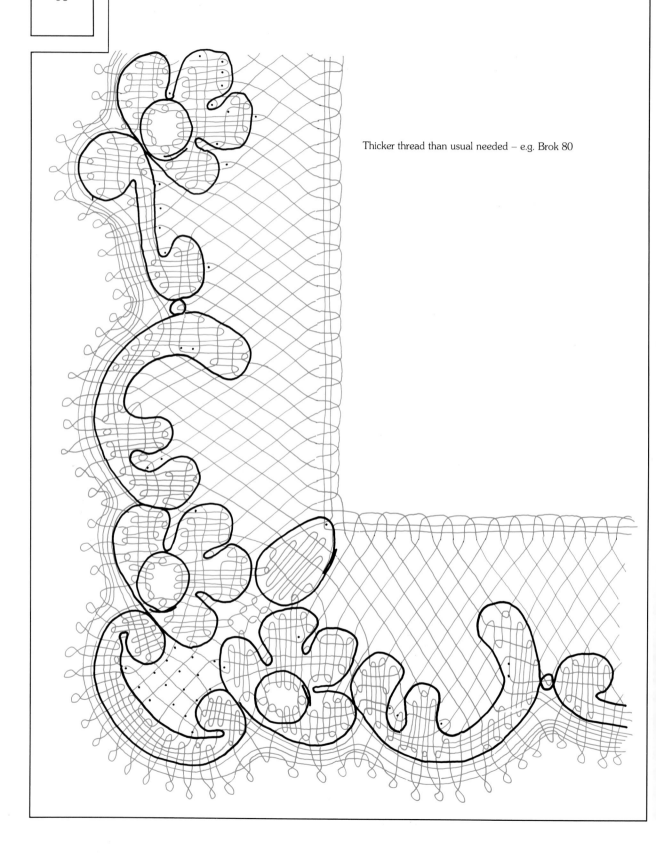

Thicker thread than usual needed – e.g. Brok 80

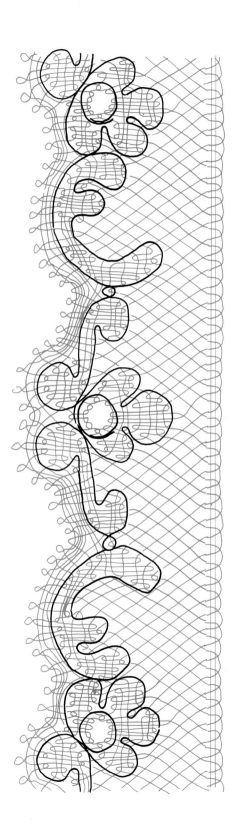

Thicker thread than usual needed – e.g. Brok 80

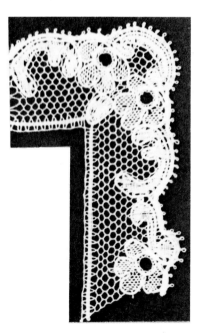

31 CAROLE – DO-IT-YOURSELF COLLAR

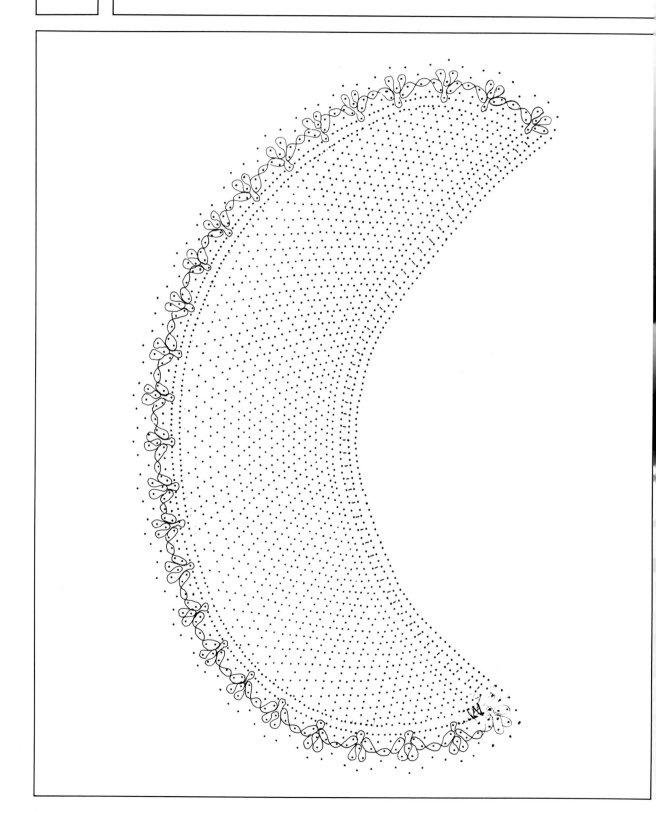

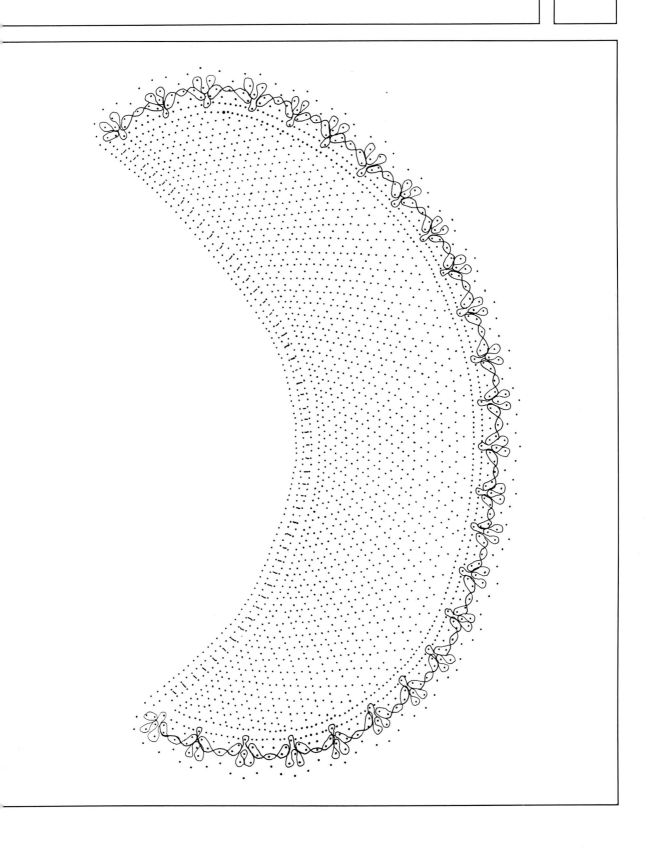

Carole Collar

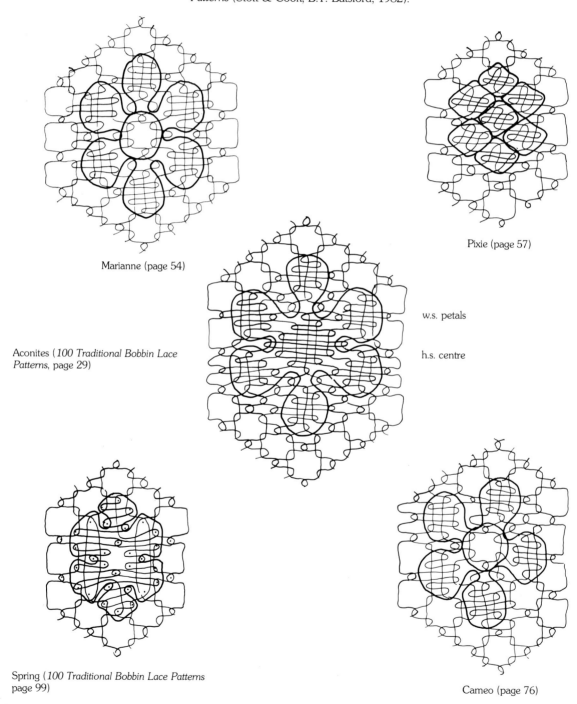

Five flower designs for Carole – three from this book and two from *100 Traditional Bobbin Lace Patterns* (Stott & Cook, B.T. Batsford, 1982).

Marianne (page 54)

Pixie (page 57)

Aconites (*100 Traditional Bobbin Lace Patterns*, page 29)

w.s. petals

h.s. centre

Spring (*100 Traditional Bobbin Lace Patterns* page 99)

Cameo (page 76)

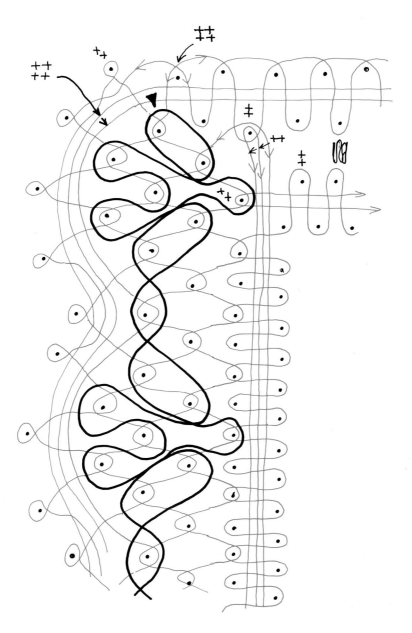

I have provided a honeycomb grid and several types of
flowers. *You* decide which flower and where to dot them
over the grid, to produce your own unique collar.

32 LILAC

Bobbins 25 pairs – **Gimps** 1 pair

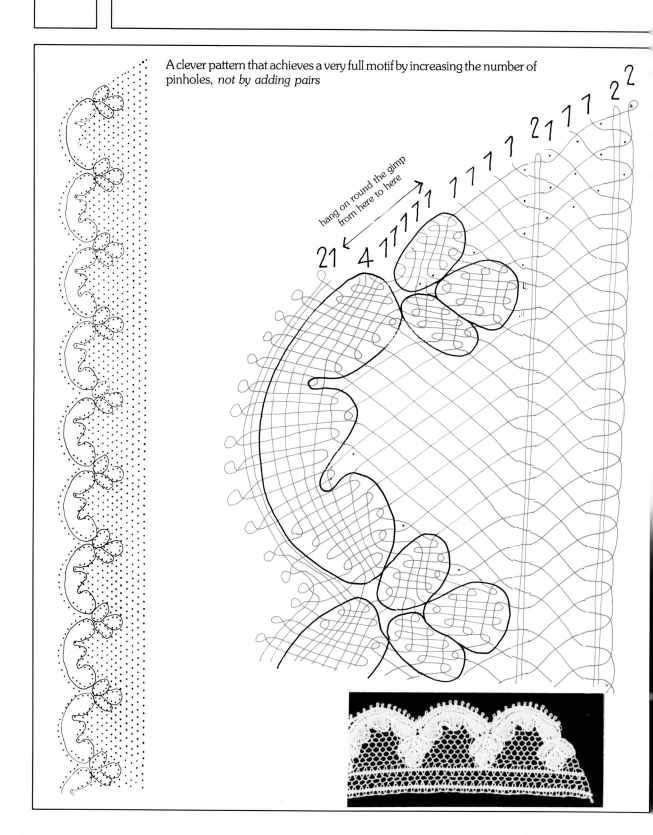

A clever pattern that achieves a very full motif by increasing the number of pinholes, *not by adding pairs*

hang on round the gimp from here to here

It pays to observe and learn from the past

I would never have guessed there were two rows of passives – double footside – if there had not been a small sample attached to the pricking. I would have just assumed it was a badly pricked ground. Also note the original lacemaker has improved on the pricking by ignoring some of the pinholes near the headside, showing the pricking does not necessarily have the perfect answer.

Do not slavishly copy and churn out immaculate, machine-like lace

Notes about working out floral patterns

Top Leaf – you will see there are pins that have no stitch round them; they are only there to help to keep the shape of the leaf – this is a very common practice.

Central Leaf – there are three possible ways to work this one (1) the rather lopsided version, as sample; (2) the double pairs end up in the wrong place for continuing the ground; (3) the method I have seen elsewhere and recommend; it is neater and fuller and the double pairs finish in a good position.

Note well the way the pairs from the headside all gather into the top of the next leaf – this is a very typical process; it is far better to have extra pairs in the work, rather than in the heading. This is only possible when there is a continuous motif at this point.

Another method of heading picots in valley

Picot A – 3 w.s. out, picot, 1 w.s. back, leave
Picot B – 4 w.s. out, picot, 1 w.s. back, leave
Picot C – 5 w.s. out, picot, 2 w.s. back, leave

Now proceed as usual.

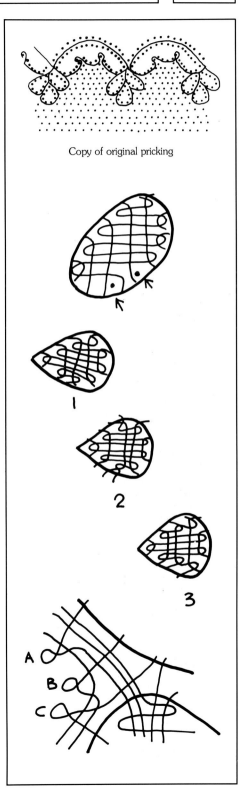

Copy of original pricking

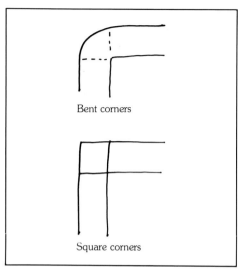

Bent corners

Square corners

I would be very rich if I had a penny every time I was asked 'Will there be corners?' There is a general fear of them, which is quite unnecessary.

Remember 'corners' are a relatively modern invention for Bucks Point lace; up till the 1930s lace was made in continuous lengths and then gathered round the corners. This looks very pretty, especially if there is a high proportion of net. Another method, instead of gathering, is to overlap and sew together. I did this once with the design called Wedding Bells and it looked good.

Design your own. Not so easy, bearing in mind the overall shape of the corner is so important. The easiest is a 'bent' corner but this is unsatisfactory visually. It is best to try and keep a shape as near square as possible – the extra blob on the Olney Handkerchief I think looks very good.

Draw out rough sketches of the whole design and pin them up on a far wall if possible. Keep looking from a distance – it's amazing how different it will look.

Another handy hint is hold the design in front of a mirror; it's surprising how this will help you to decide which you like the best.

Four neat ways round internal corner, depending on your pricking

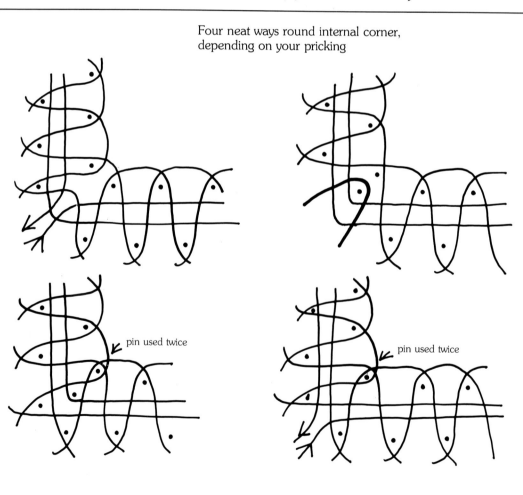

pin used twice

pin used twice

33 YVONNE

Bobbins 23 pairs – **Gimps** 3 pairs

The inspiration for this pattern came from a piece of machine lace.

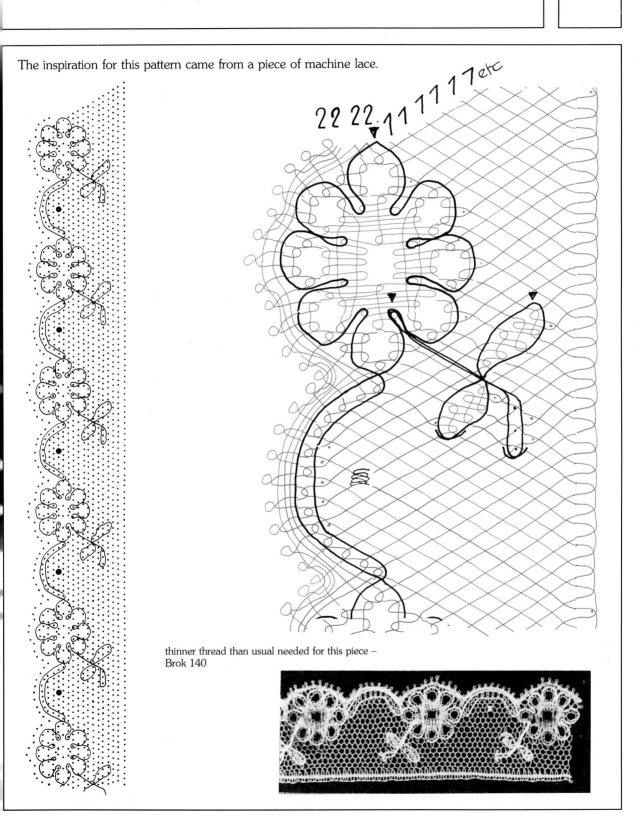

2 2 22 1 1 1 1 1 1 etc

thinner thread than usual needed for this piece –
Brok 140

34 CAMEO

Bobbins 30 pairs + 3 pairs for corner – **Gimps** 3 single + 3 pairs for corner

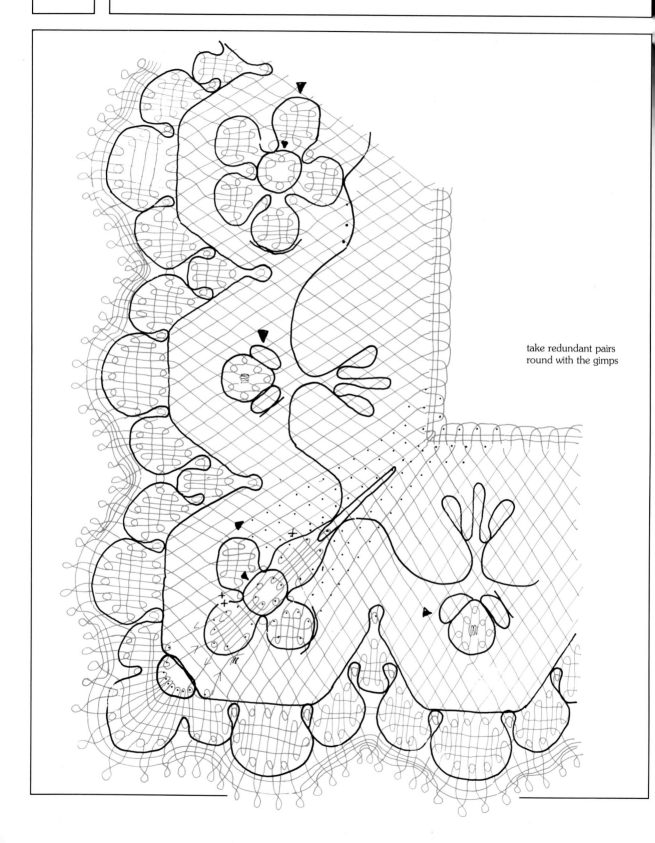

take redundant pairs
round with the gimps

35 WATERLILY
Bobbins 48 pairs – **Gimps** 5 pairs

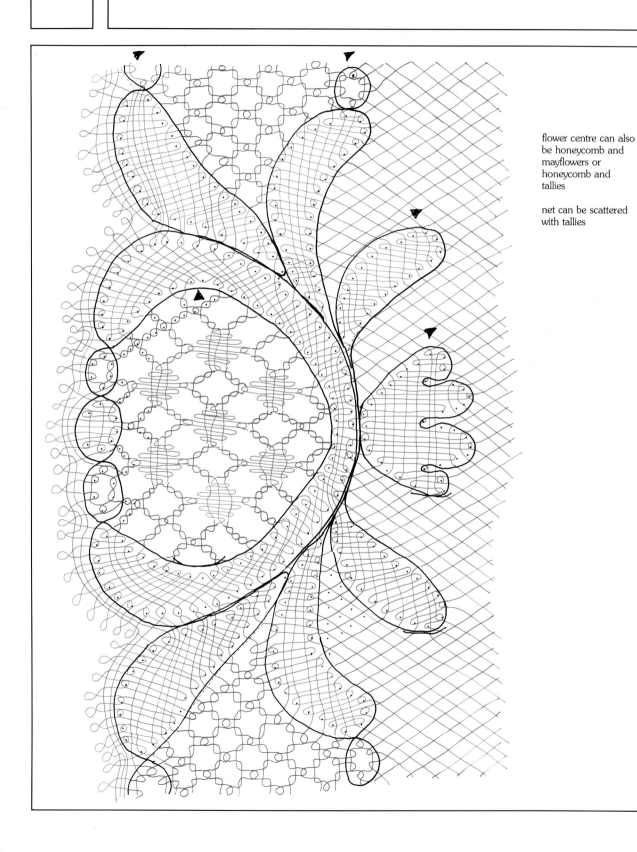

flower centre can also
be honeycomb and
mayflowers or
honeycomb and
tallies

net can be scattered
with tallies

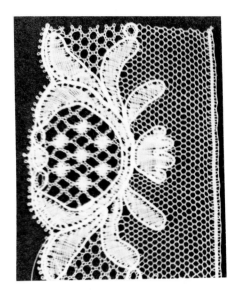

There are many versions of this very famous pattern. I have chosen a version I consider looks most like a waterlily, and have picked good techniques from many samples to get this successful hybrid.

36 APPLE BLOSSOM

'Restless' lace – where pairs are continuously added and removed

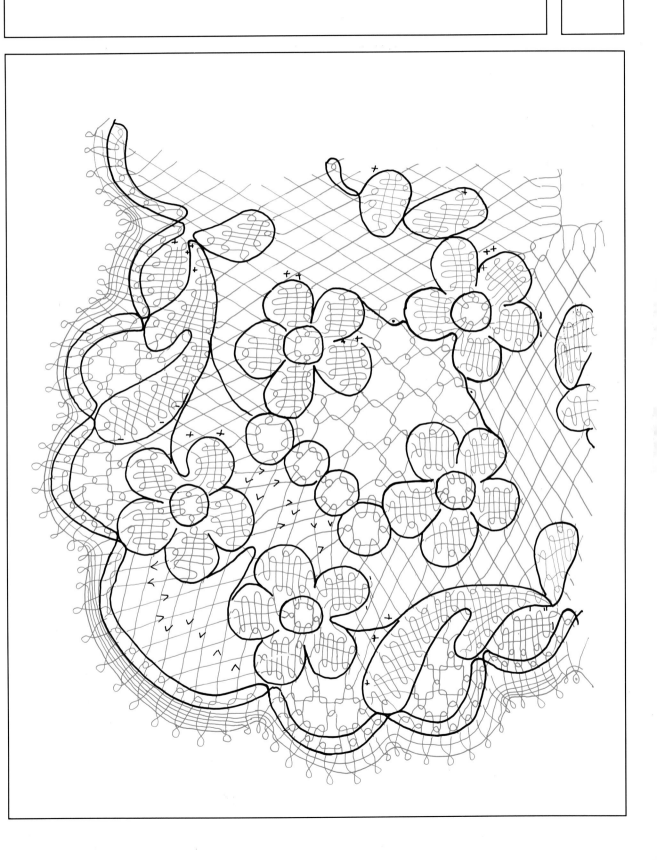

Apple Blossom

This very pretty type of Bucks Point lace I call 'Restless' lace. Pairs are constantly being added and removed – this is the only way to achieve the necessary fullness to the flowers and leaves.

It is impossible to calculate *how many pairs* are needed. The diagrams are for your guidance to show it can be done – every lacemaker will interpret it differently. I do still recommend you make notes of your variations, so you can repeat them next time!

Not a very good subject for *demonstrating* as there are so many ends obscuring the finished work. *Do not* attempt to cut off these ends before there is plenty of pinless space. Equally, take extra care when *removing pins*; the thrown back threads, especially the single gimps are in great danger of being pulled with the pins at this stage.

It will be noted from the diagrams that there are many *point ground stitches without pins* to get the threads from one area to another.

> **Grouped heading** – this bunches the vast number of passives at the heading into a much narrower width, which is sometimes desirable.

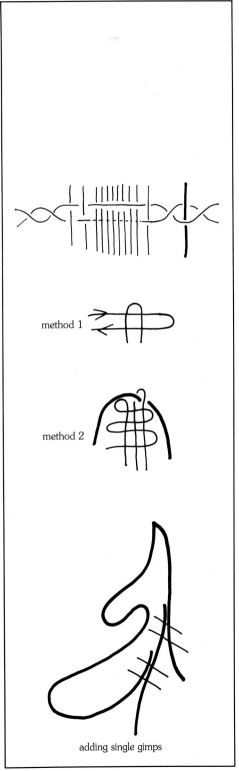

method 1

method 2

adding single gimps

Take the worker through gimp, tw.1, w.s., then pick up L.H. bobbin, take all but last pair through this gap, w.s. last pair, work picot, 1 w.s. back and thread through the rest again, w.s. tw.1 and take through gimp.

Hanging on extra pairs – There are two methods commonly used – (1) hanging over worker just before the pin; (2) hanging over the gimp. Both have their merits.

Run excess pairs round with gimps, until needed. This happens twice in the honeycomb stem areas. When adding a single gimp it is best to add it inside existing gimp a few stitches before it is needed.

Using pin twice at footside corners

Work footside pin as normal the first time, *but* do not tw.4 outside pair. When corner has been turned, work footside stitch, carefully remove the pin and pin under both new outside pairs.

37 LACES FOR RIBBON

Bobbins 9 pairs or 6 pairs and 1 pair gimps

This little piece of lace I found by accident on a lace sample in a museum. The sewing on was so skilful that you could not see the join – except at the end, where it had started to become unpicked. It is useful for sewing to edges of existing lace to make it detachable, for instance on to the Linda collar. It has no footside to help make the sewing invisible, just three twists round the pin. Sew to the footside of lace, then thread thin ribbon or silken cord through the loops. It is best to double back the first and last repeat to make a strong edging.

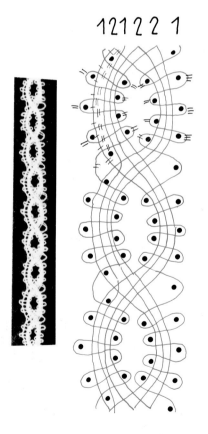

121 2 2 1

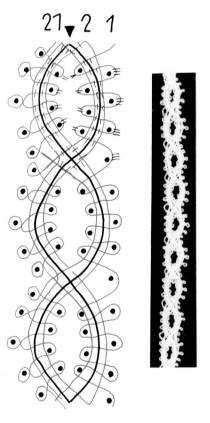

2 1 2 1

Can also be made with a gimp and picots.

38 VERONICA

Bobbins 30 pairs – **Gimps** 7 pairs (only 3 pairs in use at one time)

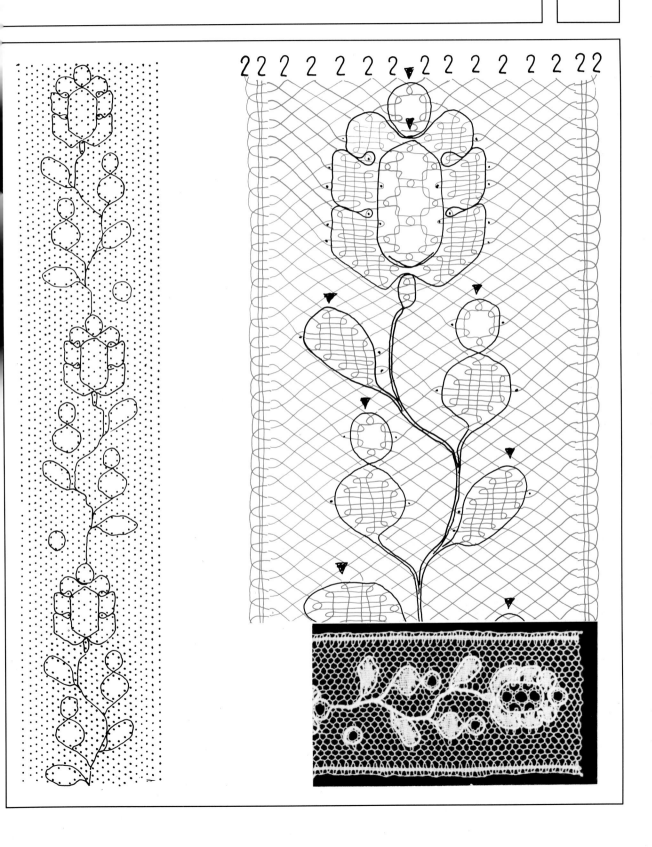

39 CORNER PRICKINGS

Corners for Marianne (see page 54) and Honeycomb Rings (see pages 8 and 9)

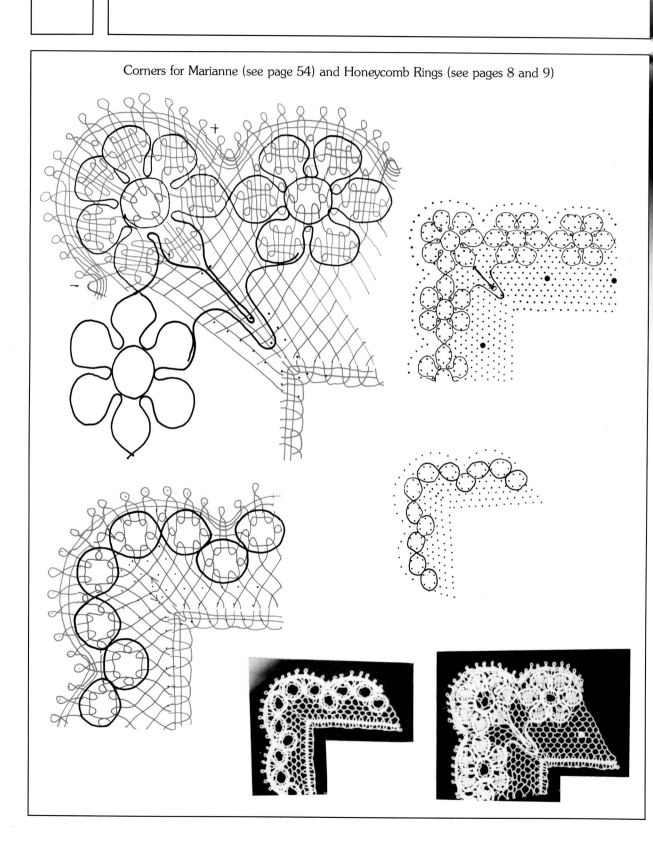

BOOK SUPPLIERS

ENGLAND

The following are stockists of the complete Batsford/Dryad Press range:

Avon
Bridge Bookshop
7 Bridge Street
Bath BA2 4AS

Waterstone & Co.
4–5 Milsom Street
Bath BA1 1DA

Bedfordshire
Arthur Sells
Lane Cover
49 Pedley Lane
Clifton
Shefford SG17 5QT

Berkshire
Loricraft
4 Big Lane
Lambourn

West End Lace Supplies
Ravensworth Court
Road
Mortimer West End
Reading RG7 3UD

Buckinghamshire
J. S. Sear
Lacecraft Supplies
8 Hillview
Sherington MK16 9NJ

Cambridgeshire
Dillons the Bookstore
Sidney Street
Cambridge

Cheshire
Lynn Turner
Church Meadow Crafts
7 Woodford Road
Winsford

Cornwall
Creative Books
22A River Street
Truro TR1 2SJ

Devon
Creative Crafts &
Needlework
18 High Street
Totnes TQ9 5NP

Honiton Lace Shop
44 High Street
Honiton EX14 8PJ

Dorset
F. Herring & Sons
27 High West Street
Dorchester DT1 1UP

Tim Parker (mail order)
124 Corhampton Road
Boscombe East
Bournemouth BH6
5NZ

Christopher Williams
19 Morrison Avenue
Parkstone
Poole BH17 4AD

Durham
Lacemaid
6, 10 & 15 Stoneybeck
Bishop Middleham
DL17 9BL

Gloucestershire
Southgate Handicrafts
63 Southgate Street
Gloucester GL1 1TX

Waterstone & Company
89–90 The Promenade
Cheltenham GL50
1NB

Hampshire
Creative Crafts
11 The Square
Winchester SO23 9ES

Doreen Gill
14 Barnfield Road
Petersfield GU31 4DR

Larkfield Crafts
4 Island Cottages
Mapledurwell
Basingstoke RG23
2LU

Needlestyle
24–26 West Street
Alresford

Ruskins
27 Bell Street
Romsey

Isle of Wight
Busy Bobbins
Unit 7
Scarrots Lane
Newport PO30 1JD

Kent
The Handicraft Shop
47 Northgate
Canterbury CT1 1BE

Hatchards
The Great Hall
Mount Pleasant Road
Tunbridge Wells

London
W. & G. Foyle Ltd
113–119 Charing Cross
Road WC2H 0EB

Hatchards
187 Piccadilly W1V
9DA

Middlesex
Redburn Crafts
Squires Garden Centre
Halliford Road
Upper Halliford
Shepperton TW17
8RU

Norfolk
Alby Lace Museum
Cromer Road
Alby
Norwich NR11 7QE

Jane's Pincushions
Taverham Craft Unit 4
Taverham Nursery
Centre
Fir Covert Road
Taverham
Norwich NR8 6HT

Waterstone & Co.
30 London Street
Norwich NR2 1LD

Northamptonshire
Denis Hornsby
149 High Street
Burton Latimer
Kettering NN15 5RL

Somerset
Bridge Bookshop
62 Bridge Street
Taunton TA1 1UD

Staffordshire
J. & J. Ford (mail order
& lace days only)
October Hill
Upper Way
Upper Longdon
Rugeley WS15 1QB

Sussex
Waterstone & Co.
120 Terminus Road
Eastbourne

Warwickshire
Christine & David
Springett
21 Hillmorton Road
Rugby CV22 6DF

Wiltshire
Everyman Bookshop
5 Bridge Street
Salisbury SP1 2ND

North Yorkshire
Craft Basics
9 Gillygate
York

Shireburn Lace
Finkle Court
Finkle Hill
Sherburn in Elmet
LS25 6EB

The Craft House
23 Bar Street
Scarborough YO13
9QE

West Midlands
Needlewoman
21 Needles Alley
off New Street
Birmingham B2 5AE

West Yorkshire
Sebalace
Waterloo Mill
Howden Road
Silsden BD20 0HA

George White
Lacemaking
Supplies
40 Heath Drive
Boston Spa LS23 6PB

Just Lace
14 Ashwood Gardens
Gildersome
Leeds LS27 7AS

Jo Firth
58 Kent Crescent
Lowtown, Pudsey
Leeds LS28 9EB

SCOTLAND

Central Scotland Lace
Supplies
3 Strude Howe
Alva
Clack's FK12 5JU

Embroidery Shop
51 William Street
Edinburgh
Lothian EH3 7LW

Waterstone & Co.
236 Union Street
Aberdeen AB1 1TN

WALES

Bryncraft Bobbins (mail
order)
B. J. Phillips
Pantglas
Cellan
Lampeter
Dyfed SA48 BJD

Hilkar Lace Suppliers
33 Mysydd Road
Landore
Swansea

EQUIPMENT SUPPLIERS

UNITED KINGDOM

Bedfordshire
A. Sells
49 Pedley Lane
Clifton
Shefford SG17 5QT

Berkshire
Chrisken Bobbins
26 Cedar Drive
Kingsclere RG15 8TD

Loricraft (general and
bobbins)
4 Big Lane
Lambourn

West End Lace Supplies
(general and
bobbins)
Ravensworth Court
Road
Mortimer West End
Reading RG7 3UD

Buckinghamshire
Bartlett, Caesar and
Partners (bobbins
and lace pillows)
12 Creslow Court
Stony Stratford
Milton Keynes MK11
1NN

J. S. Sear
Lacecraft Supplies
8 Hillview
Sherington MK16 9NJ

Sizelands
1 Highfield Road
Winslow MK10 3QU

SMP
4 Garners Close
Chalfont St Peter SL9
0HB

Cambridgeshire
Heffers Graphic Shop
(matt coloured
transparent
adhesive film)
26 King Street
Cambridge CB1 1LN

Ken & Pat Schultz
134 Wisbech Road
Thornley
Peterborough

Spangles
Carole Morris
Cashburn Lane
Burwell CB5 0ED

Cheshire
Lynn Turner
Church Meadow Crafts
7 Woodford Road
Winsford

Devon
Honiton Lace Shop
44 High Street
Honiton EX14 8PJ

Dorset
Frank Herring & Sons
27 High West Street
Dorchester DT1 1UP

T. Parker (mail order,
general and
bobbins)
124 Corhampton Road
Boscombe East
Bournemouth BH6
5NZ

Essex
Needlework
Ann Bartleet
Bucklers Farm
Coggeshall CO6 1SB

Gloucestershire
T. Brown (bobbins)
Temple Lane Cottage
Littledean
Cinderford

Chosen Crafts Centre
46 Winchcombe Street
Cheltenham GL52
2ND

Hampshire
Bartlett, Caesar and
Partners (bobbins
and lace pillows)
The Glen
Shorefield Road
Downton
Lymington SO41 0LH

Busy Bobbins
Unit 7
Scarrots Lane
Newport IOW PO30
1JD

Larkfield Crafts
(bobbins)
Hilary Ricketts
4 Island Cottages
Mapledurwell
Basingstoke RG25
2LU

Needlestyle
24–26 West Street
Alresford

Newnham Lace
Equipment (lace
pillows)
15 Marlowe Close
Basingstoke RG24
9DD

Richard Viney (bobbins)
Unit 7
Port Royal Street
Southsea PO5 3UD

Kent
The Handicraft Shop
47 Northgate
Canterbury CT1 1BE

Denis Hornsby
25 Manwood Avenue
Canterbury CT2 7AH

Frances Iles
73 High Street
Rochester ME1 1LX

Lancashire
Malcolm J. Fielding
(bobbins)
2 Northern Terrace
Moss Lane
Silverdale LA5 0ST

Merseyside
Hayes & Finch
Head Office & Factory
Hanson Road
Aintree
Liverpool L9 9BP

Middlesex
Redburn Crafts
Squires Garden Centre
Halliford Road
Upper Halliford
Shepperton TW17
8RU

Norfolk
Alby Lace Museum
Cromer Road
Alby
Norwich NR11 7QE

Jane's Pincushions
Taverham Craft Unit 4
Taverham Nursery
Centre
Fir Covert Road
Taverham
Norwich NR8 6HT

Jane Playford
North Lodge
Church Close
West Runton NR27
9QY

George Walker
The Corner Shop
Rickinghall, Diss

North Humberside
Teazle Embroideries
35 Boothferry Road
Hull

North Yorkshire
The Craft House
23 Bar Street
Scarborough

Shireburn Lace
Finkle Court
Finkle Hill
Sherburn in Elmet
LS25 6EB

Stitchery
Finkle Street
Richmond

Northants
Denis Hornsby
149 High Street
Burton Latimer
Kettering   NN15 5RL

SCOTLAND
Central Scotland Lace
   Supplies
3 Strude Howe
Clack's   FK12 5JU

Christine Riley
53 Barclay Street
Stonehaven
Kincardineshire

Peter & Beverley Scarlett
Strupak
Hill Head
Cold Wells, Ellon
Grampian

South Yorkshire
D. H. Shaw
47 Lamor Crescent
Thrushcroft
Rotherham   S66 9QD

Staffordshire
J. & J. Ford (*mail order
   and lace days only*)
October Hill
Upper Way
Upper Longdon
Rugeley   WS15 1QB

Suffolk
A. R. Archer (*bobbins*)
The Poplars
Shetland
near Stowmarket   IP14
   3DE

Mary Collins (*linen by
   the metre, and
   made up articles of
   church linen*)
Church Furnishings
St Andrews Hall
Humber Doucy Lane
Ipswich   IP4 3BP

E. & J. Piper (*silk
   embroidery and
   lace thread*)
Silverlea
Flax Lane
Glemsford   CO10 7RS

Surrey
Needle and Thread
80 High Street
Horsell
Woking   GU21 4SZ

Needlestyle
5 The Woolmead
Farnham   GU9 7TX

Sussex
Southern Handicrafts
20 Kensington Gardens
Brighton   BN1 4AC

WALES
Bryncraft Bobbins
B. J. Phillips
Pantglas
Cellan
Lampeter
Dyfed   SA48 BJD

Hilkar Lace Suppliers
33 Mysydd Road
Landore
Swansea

Warwickshire
Christine & David
   Springett
21 Hillmorton Road
Rugby   CV22 5DF

West Midlands
Framecraft
83 Hampstead Road
Handsworth Wood
Birmingham   B2 1JA

Framecraft Miniatures
   Ltd (*frames and
   mounts*)
148–150 High Street
Aston
Birmingham   B6 4US

The Needlewoman
21 Needles Alley
off New Street
Birmingham   B2 5AE

Stitches
Dovehouse Shopping
   Parade
Warwick Road
Olton, Solihull

West Yorkshire
Jo Firth
Lace Marketing &
   Needlecraft
   Supplies
58 Kent Crescent
Lowtown
Pudsey   LS28 9EB

Just Lace
Lacemaker Supplies
14 Ashwood Gardens
Gildersome
Leeds   LS27 7AS

Sebalace
Waterloo Mills
Howden Road
Silsden   BD2 0NA

George White
   Lacemaking
   Supplies
40 Heath Drive
Boston Spa   LS23 6PB

Wiltshire
Doreen Campbell
   (*frames and
   mounts*)
Highcliff
Bremilham Road
Malmesbury   SN16
   0DQ

Worcestershire
Richard Gravestock
   (*general and
   bobbins*)
Highwood
Crews Hill
Alfrick   WR6 5HF

AUSTRALIA
Australian Lace
   magazine
P.O. Box 1291
Toowong
Queensland 4066

Dentelles Lace Supplies
c/o Betty Franks
39 Lang Terrace
Northgate 4013
Brisbane
Queensland

The Lacemaker
94 Fordham Avenue
Hartwell
Victoria 3124

Spindle and Loom
Arcade 83
Longueville Road
Lane Cove
NSW 2066

Tulis Crafts
201 Avoca Street
Randwick
NSW 2031

BELGIUM
't Handwerkhuisje
Katelijnestraat 23
8000 Bruges

Kantcentrum
Balstraat 14
8000 Bruges

Manufacture Belge de
   Dentelle
6 Galerie de la Reine
Galeries Royales St
   Hubert
1000 Bruxelles

Orchidée
Mariastraat 18
8000 Bruges

Ann Thys
't Apostelientje
Balstraat 11
8000 Bruges

FRANCE
Centre d'Initiations à la
   Dentelle du Puy
2 Rue Duguesclin
43000 Le Puy en Vela

A L'Econome
Anne-Marie Deydier
Ecole de Dentelle aux
   Fuseaux
10 rue Paul Chenavard
69001 Lyon

Rougier and Plé
13–15 Bd des Filles de
   Calvaire
75003 Paris

WEST GERMANY
Der Fenster Laden
Berliner Str. 8
D 6483 Bad Soden
Salmünster

P. P. Hempel
Ortolanweg 34
1000 Berlin

HOLLAND
Blokker's Boektiek
Bronsteeweg 4/4a
2101 AC Heemstede

Theo Brejaart
Dordtselaan 146–148
P.O. Box 5199
3008 AD Rotterdam

Heikina de Ruÿter
Zuiderstraat 1
9693 ER Niewenschans

Magazijn *De Vlijt*
Lijnmarkt 48
Utrecht

SWITZERLAND
Fadehax
Inh. Irene Solca
4105 Biel-Benken
Basel

NEW ZEALAND
Peter McLeavey
P.O. Box 69.007
Auckland 8

USA
Arbor House
22 Arbor Lane
Roslyn Heights
NY 11577

Baltazor Inc.
3262 Severn Avenue
Metairie
LA 7002

Beggars' Lace
P.O. Box 17263
Denver
Colo 80217

Berga Ullman Inc.
P.O. Box 918
North Adams
MA 01247

Frederick J. Fawcett
129 South Street
Boston
MA 02130

Frivolité
15526 Densmore N.
Seattle
WA 98113

Happy Hands
3007 S. W. Marshall
Pendleton
Oreg 97180

International Old Lacers
P.O. Box 1029
Westminster
Colo 80030

Lace Place de Belgique
800 S. W. 17th Street
Boca Raton
FL 33432

Lacis
2150 Stuart Street
Berkeley
CA 9470

Robin's Bobbins
RTL Box 1736
Mineral Bluff
GA 30559

Robin and Russ
Handweavers
533 North Adams Street
McMinnvills
Oreg 97128

Some Place
2990 Adline Street
Berkeley
CA 94703

Osma G. Todd Studio
319 Mendoza Avenue
Coral Gables
FL 33134

The Unique And Art
Lace Cleaners
5926 Delman Boulevard
St Louis
MO 63112

Van Scriver Bobbin Lace
130 Cascadilla Park
Ithaca
NY 14850

The World in Stitches
82 South Street
Milford
N.H. 0305

SOURCES OF
INFORMATION

UNITED KINGDOM
The British College of
   Lace
21 Hillmorton Road
Rugby
War   CV22 5DF

The English Lace School
Oak House
Church Stile
Woodbury
Nr. Exeter
Devon   EX5 1HP

The Lace Guild
The Hollies
53 Audnam
Stourbridge
West Midlands   DY8
   4AE

The Lacemakers' Circle
49 Wardwick
Derby   DE1 1HY

The Lace Society
Linwood
Stratford Road
Oversley
Alcester
War   BY9 6PG

Ring of Tatters
Mrs Gwenda Partridge
7 Town Head Avenue
Settle
N. Yorks   BD24 9RQ

United Kingdom Director
   of International Old
   Lacers
S. Hurst
4 Dollis Road
London N3 1RG

USA
International Old Lacers
Gunvor Jorgensen
   (Pres.)
366 Bradley Avenue
Northvale
NR 076647

Lace & Crafts magazine
3201 East Lakeshore
   Drive
Tallahassee
FL 32312–2034